Bill Huebsch *with* **David W**

The Pastoral Parish in the Modern World

8 Group Exercises to Teach the
New Vocabulary of Pastoral Ministry
and How to Enact It

Pastoral Ministry
Synodality
Discernment
Evangelization
Catechesis
Accompaniment
Theological Reflection
Missionary Discipleship

 Published by The Pastoral Center/PastoralCenter.com.

 The author has edited some passages of the NRSVue to render them more gender inclusive with reference to God.

Some of the elements of the prayers in each chapter are drawn from *The Echo Within* © 2023 by Bill Huebsch.

Paraphrases of documents of Vatican II are drawn from *The Story and Promise of Vatican II: in Plain English* (The Pastoral Center, 2020).

Paraphrases of the *Catechism of the Catholic Church* in plain English are drawn from *Growing Faith* (Twenty-Third Publications, 2023).

All direct quotations appear in quotation marks. All other references are summaries or paraphrases by the author (such as those referenced above) and are drawn from the document cited.

The principles and guidelines for pastoral theology are drawn from *Promise and Hope: Pastoral Theology in the Age of Mercy* (Twenty-Third Publications, 2020). Used with permission.

Some of the remarks in the chapter on accompaniment are excerpted from *The Art of Accompaniment* (Twenty-Third Publications, 2017).

The discussion of pastoral theology here is inspired by and drawn in part from a speech delivered by San Diego Bishop-now-a-Cardinal Bob McElroy at the 2018 assembly of the Association of U.S. Catholic Priests meeting in Albuquerque. That speech was entitled "Pastoral Theology for a Post-Modern World."

Material on evangelization, catechesis, and accompaniment is drawn from the *Group Reading Guide for Evangelii Gaudium (The Joy of the Gospel)* (Twenty-Third Publications, 2013) and *The Group Reading Guide for Amoris Laetitia (The Joy of Love)* (Twenty-Third Publications, 2016)

ISBN 978-1-949628-29-6

Contents

Introduction

The pastoral ministry lexicon of the Catholic Church is filled with terms that not everyone understands. One evening several years ago in a parish hall, a very earnest young woman in training to be a catechist stood to ask a question. She was wondering what we meant by the word "catechesis." In my best Socratic style, I asked her what she thought it meant. She looked at me over the small group gathered to study whole community catechesis and said quietly, "Well, I thought it was a disease of the skin."

Oh my.

A new pastoral vocabulary keeps evolving as the Church moves forward and advances its understanding of how best to enact the ministry of Jesus in the modern world. I'm quite sure this young woman would have easily recognized the now-defunct term "catechism class," but we have moved on, and we speak only of catechesis these days.

Recently, we have added the vocabulary of "accompaniment" and its cousin, "theological reflection." The latter term has been widely used in the past but not by most laypeople. The person who enacts accompaniment might be called an accompanist, but that term suggests mainly a piano player for most people.

In the 2020s, we have heard much talk about "synods," "synodality," and "synodal." Sometimes we hear about "the spirit of synodality." Unlike the terms accompanist or catechesis, the term "synod" leaves most people a bit blank. It's just not a word we use very often, if at all.

Pastoral theology anew

All these terms, among others, fit into the larger envelope called "pastoral ministry." As now-cardinal Bob McElroy of San Diego said in a speech in 2018, "We are seeing an emerging pastoral theology at the very heart of the life of the Church." This theology connects us to the pastoral style of Jesus and is adapted to the challenges and cultures of the modern world.

In that speech, he said that this emerging pastoral outlook "demands that all the other branches of theology attend to the concrete reality of human life and suffering in a much more substantial way in forming doctrine.

"It states that the lived experience of human sinfulness and human conversion is vital to understanding the central attribute of God concerning us, which is mercy.

"It demands that moral theology proceed from the actual pastoral action of Jesus Christ, which does not first demand a change of life but begins with an embrace of divine love, proceeds to the action of healing, and only then requires a conversion" in responsible conscience.

The new pastoral theology calls on us to make sure that the rules and style of our liturgy "be formed in a compassionate embrace with the often-overwhelming life challenges which prevent men and women at periods of their life from conforming adequately with important gospel challenges. [It] rejects a notion of law which can be blind to the uniqueness of concrete human situations, suffering, and limitation."

We can plainly see that the practices of shared decision-making, accompanying one another, helping each other reflect theologically, catechizing, witnessing, discerning, inviting, welcoming, and pastoring are much needed.

Hence, the new terms we use

These are exciting times in the Church as we continue to deepen our theology and reconnect it to Christ's radiant and luminous presence within and among us. How to understand the Holy Mystery of this generous, divine presence leads us to this constantly new vocabulary as we describe pastoral ministry. We should all understand these terms and how they are enacted in our work. And we should share in a common understanding within each parish. Hence this workbook.

We now speak often of practices such as "mystagogy," a term which only recently had not been used in common church parlance for a long time. In plain English, it means that we look back over our shoulders to review our experience of liturgy or life and peer into it to find the mysterious hand of God, figuratively speaking. Only when we look back do we recognize how God has touched our hearts.

Likewise, the recent Jubilee of Mercy taught us to use the term "mercy" to describe the very face of God, figuratively speaking. "Mercy cannot become a mere parenthesis in the life of the Church," Pope Francis wrote in his apostolic letter *Misericordia et Misera*. Mercy is what the Church is made of, he said. "And only through mercy are the profound truths of the Gospel made manifest and tangible. Everything is revealed in mercy; everything is resolved in the merciful love of the Father."

Those who work in pastoral ministry

At one time not so long ago in our parishes, the only ministers were either ordained or, occasionally, a religious sister. But today, many lay people are ready to take up the work of pastoral ministry. In some parts of the Church, thousands of lay pastoral ministers are already working at nearly every level of parish life. We are on the horizon of that reality in other parts of the Church as the clergy age and parish needs change. This makes it even more important that we fully understand the terminology and tasks to which we are being called.

We are being called to **pastoral ministry** first and foremost, so knowing what that means is essential. We're also being called to be **synodal**, to listen, walk together, and discern to what God may be calling us as a parish or even as the wider church. We're being asked to engage in **evangelization**—which many Catholics once considered a mainly Protestant enterprise.

I've already mentioned catechesis, but we're also being challenged today by the 2020 *Directory for Catechesis* to put the **kerygma** front and center in all faith formation. The kerygma? Hmmm…another new term. The kerygma is the core message of the Good News: Jesus loves and cares for you. He knows your heart. He demonstrated his love by his self-giving death on the cross. Now he accompanies you in your daily life. This "kerygmatic" message, as the *Directory* and *The Joy of the Gospel* remind us, should be the first words on the lips of every catechist, ringing out over and over.

We're likewise called to embrace a **catechumenal model** of catechesis. Indeed, the *Directory* I just cited tells us in its introduction that the Catechumenate should inspire all catechesis. We're not to be blamed for being unsure what this means because, until Vatican II's 1963 *Constitution on Liturgy*, #64, the catechumenate had not been widely used since the 4th century. This model suggests three stages in faith formation. First, to meet and know Christ, to turn our hearts to Christ, and to center our lives on that. Second, with that burning faith in our hearts, to study the Catholic faith and celebrate its liturgies. And third, to engage in mystagogy, which I described above.

Likewise, we're being insistently called to put **accompaniment** into practice throughout pastoral ministry. We're called to become companions for one another and help one another discern to what God may be calling us in the specific concrete situations of our lives. This leads to opening doors, removing barriers, and offering a warm welcome. A principal tool in accompaniment is **theological reflection**, which we must all learn to enact. And, finally, we're called today to act as **missionary disciples**. We may have once thought that all missionaries worked in "foreign lands," but today, that missionary work also includes our own land. What does this mean for us?

Whew! It's all a lot to wrap our minds around. A newly emerging pastoral theology and ministry. Synodality, along with listening and shared decision-making. Discernment as an element of all this work. Evangelization as the primary goal of the Church in every ministry and sacrament. Catechesis, the catechumenal model, the kerygma, and mystagogy, not to mention the role of parents and the need for lifelong learning. Becoming companions in accompaniment. Using theological reflection. Being a missionary disciple. Whew!

Not to worry, dear reader. The workbook you're reading is a tool to help us learn the new vocabulary of pastoral ministry and know how to enact it.

Our method in this workbook

This workbook has eight exercises—one for each of eight topics in the new vocabulary of pastoral ministry. Every leader, including the ordained and long-time workers, should be part of this learning process.

1. There is a brief amount of preparatory self-study, which we suggest each participant do before the parish meeting.
2. There follows the wider parish gathering in which everyone's ideas will be collected together and developed further.
3. The result will be a pastoral plan for each facet of pastoral ministry under study.

SELF-STUDY IN PREPARATION FOR THE PARISH MEETING

1. Begin with prayer. We provide a suggested one, or you may choose one of your own.
2. Each pastoral topic is defined in plain English. Please study this definition and be ready to restate it in your own words. We provide a brief video clip setting the stage for each topic. These clips can be viewed on any device.
3. There follows a brief explanation of how each topic fits into the church's life. We invite you to read and reflect on the church's teaching about each.
4. In closing, there is a brief period for theological reflection.

SUGGESTIONS FOR THE PARISH MEETING

1. We suggest you begin the wider parish gathering with a brief prayer, and we have provided that for you.
2. For each exercise, follow the simple steps we have outlined, and please allow plenty of time for everyone to speak.
3. Sometimes, finishing the work in one meeting won't be possible. Please be open to continuing your conversations later in follow-up meetings.
4. We suggest you record specific, concrete ideas to implement each of the eight topics of pastoral ministry under study. This will form and shape your eventual pastoral plan.

GUIDELINES FOR YOUR CONVERSATION

1. Please speak with courtesy and charity while also speaking openly and honestly.
2. Please put aside defensive reactions to any area of ministry under discussion. We aim to improve how we do the work of the Reign of God, not to criticize current programs.
3. Please guard against allowing anyone to dominate your discussion. This process will succeed when we hear from many people. In settings with many participants, it won't be possible for everyone to speak unless you break into smaller groups.

Prayer Before Each Exercise

Quietly, meditatively, and slowly

Prepare yourself for this by quieting your heart and mind. Settle in comfortably, and do not rush. If prayed in community, alternate readers with each stanza. A hymn may be sung as you begin. Set aside all other concerns for the moment and, when you are ready, begin with the Sign of the Cross.

Opening Prayer

Please pray this in unison.

O God, we know that you are with us
and that you are present in all we do.
As we gather to build your Church
by the Light of the Holy Spirit,
may we be generous and kind to each other,
and open to where you will lead us.
Through Christ, our Lord. Amen.

Gospel

A reading from the Gospel of Mark

James and John, the sons of Zebedee, came forward to him and said, "Teacher, we want you to do for us whatever we ask of you." And [Jesus] said to them, "What is it you want me to do for you?" And they said to him, "Appoint us to sit, one at your right hand and one at your left, in your glory." When the [others] heard this, they began to be angry with James and John. So, Jesus called them and said to them, "You know that among the gentiles, those whom they recognize as their rulers lord it over them, and their great ones are tyrants over them. But it is not so among you; instead, whoever wishes to become great among you must be your servant, and whoever wishes to be first among you must be the servant of all.

—Mark 10: 35-37, 41-44

The Gospel of the Lord
Praise to you, Lord Jesus Christ

Quiet Reflection

If you are in a group, please share your faith.

- How are you called to be a servant to others in your parish, neighborhood, family, and wider society? How does your parish serve the People of God?

- Jesus showed us how to be a servant by washing his disciples' feet at the Last Supper and by his self-giving love on the Cross. How do you "wash the feet" of others? How do you "give up your life" for others?

Concluding Prayer

Please pray this in unison.

We turn our hearts to you now
as our beloved divine companion.
We open ourselves to your presence
within and among us.
May the insights from this prayer guide us
as we work to lead this parish
and may our words and actions reflect
your generous love. Amen.

1a. Pastoral Ministry

Self-study in Preparation for the Parish Meeting

If possible, please prepare for the parish meeting with the material below.

Pastoral theology is the basket in which all the other vocabulary being studied here are gathered and enacted as "pastoral ministry."

Outcome: You will understand the meaning of the term "pastoral ministry" and how the enactment of pastoral ministry encompasses all of parish life. You will examine your own lives for how you have experienced pastoral ministry on your behalf or provided it for others.

1. Prayer

Use the prayer on the "Prayer Before Each Exercise" handout or use a prayer of your own making.

2. Definition in Plain English

What is pastoral ministry? How is it enacted in the Church?

1. View the video clip about pastoral ministry:

   https://pastoralplanning.com/ppmw-1

2. Learn this definition well enough to teach it to others.

Definition in plain English

Pastoral ministry is the group of actions we take on behalf of others to heal the hearts of women and men who are suffering, searching for a connection with the divine, or seeking holy wisdom. Such ministry constitutes the very nature of the church itself and is at the heart of all pastoral activity. Pastoral ministry always follows and reflects the pastoral style of Jesus. In all cases, pastoral ministry pays attention to the real, concrete life situations in which people live their daily lives.

EXERCISE

Cover up the definition above and write it in your own words in the space to the right.

3. Learn about Pastoral Ministry

From an interview with Pope Francis in September 2013 by Antonio Spadaro:

"I see clearly that the thing the Church needs most today is the ability to heal wounds and to warm the hearts of the faithful; it needs nearness, proximity. I see the Church as a field hospital after battle. It is useless to ask a seriously injured person if he has high cholesterol and about the level of his blood sugars. You have to heal his wounds. Then we can talk about everything else. Heal the wounds. And you have to start from the ground up. This is the mission of the Church: the Church heals, it cures.... The mission of the Church is to heal wounds of the heart, to open doors, to free people, to say that God is good, God forgives all, God is the father."

REFLECT AND SHARE

In your own words, write a brief summary of Pope Francis' teaching about pastoral ministry in the space to the left.

LEARN FROM VATICAN II

From The Constitution on the Church, *#8*

We who claim to be the Church,
we who claim to be the Body of Jesus Christ,
must resemble Christ as much as possible.
We must take the part of the poor whenever we can;
we must defend those without power;
we must avoid seeking our own glory
and act with humility and self-sacrifice for the good of all.
We who are Christian
and, indeed, the organized church itself,
must take in those who are afflicted,
forgotten,
and suffering.
The church itself, like its members,
is always in need of being renewed and forgiven,
of being purified for its mission
which is the same as the mission of Jesus.
And if we are faithful in this way as an organized church
and as its individual members,
we will succeed in announcing Jesus to the world
until all is seen in full light.

From The Constitution on the Church in the Modern World, *#1*

"The joys and hopes, the griefs and anxieties of the men and women of this age, especially those who are poor or in any way afflicted: these are the joys and hopes, the griefs and anxieties, of the followers of Christ. Indeed, nothing genuinely human fails to raise an echo in their hearts." The Christian community is, after all, a community of women and men genuinely linked with humankind and its history, bearing a message of salvation intended for all people.

REFLECT AND SHARE

Write your response to the following reflections in the space to the right.

✱ What strikes you in the two sections from Vatican II just above?

✱ What words caught your ear?

✱ How do you connect this teaching to pastoral ministry?

LEARN FROM THE CATECHISM

From articles 2052–2053

Do you remember the story in the Gospels
of the rich young man who came to see Jesus?
It is told in three of the Gospels:
Matthew, Mark, and Luke.
In Matthew, it's in chapter nineteen.
"Teacher," he asked Jesus,
"what good deed must I do, to have eternal life?"
Jesus responded by telling him simply
to keep the Commandments
and he recited a short list of them.
But the young man was restless and unsatisfied:
"I have kept all these," he said,
"what do I still lack?"
Jesus added then the demand of the Gospel.

He wasn't doing away with the Commandments
but orienting them to the Kingdom.
"If you wish to be perfect," he told the young man,
"go, sell your possessions
and give the money to the poor,
and you will have treasure in heaven.
Then, come, follow me."

Hence, Jesus increased the demand for love
on the part of this young man.

More than merely following the laws is required.
We must also go the extra mile
and Jesus taught us how to do that.

REFLECT AND SHARE

In the space to the right, list some examples from our modern times showing how we may sometimes be called to go beyond the law in order to fulfill the demands of the gospel.

How can pastoral ministry in your parish help people choose how to respond to the immigrants at our borders, the use of capital punishment, racism, personal crises of faith, family members who are no longer part of the church, and other situations?

Add your own ideas here:

4. Enacting Pastoral Ministry

Read & reflect on times and places when we enact pastoral ministry:

In our daily lives:

- Tending our aging parents
- Caring for our children and raising them in the faith
- Helping our neighbors in need
- In our daily prayer
- Taking part in movements for peace, justice, and the care of the poor
- Caring for the earth and its climate

At the parish:

- Liturgy and shared prayer
- Catechesis, education, formation, and life-long learning
- Pastoral care for the sick, dying, homebound, poor, and weak
- Welcoming and forming parish community
- Stewardship and sound financial management
- Leadership, team building, and being the pastor

5. Pastoral Ministry in Parish & Daily Life

Stories from a fellow pastoral minister:

It was the way she did it that impressed me the most. At the end of the morning, she would usher him to the front of the classroom, quietly assess his workbook, explain things, and then send him back to his desk. There was nothing remarkable about that. Except that as he returned to his seat, he was now in possession of homemade sandwiches slipped subtly into his hand during the conversation. You wouldn't see it happen if you didn't watch out for it. No one else did. Later she would investigate the cause of the apparent neglect and involve the proper agencies to support the boy. For now, though, she ensured he didn't go hungry. When I discretely asked why she was making his lunch, she said, "No one learns when they're hungry." She added, "Don't make a deal of it. It's me doing my job." I was in the presence of a good teacher with a strong sense of pastoral ministry that ensured the dignity of everyone in her class.

Stories from a fellow pastoral minister:

It was a sunny day in June when they found him. A man walking his dog came across the sorry sight. At first, he thought it was a mannequin tossed into the ditch at the side of the road. Days later, neither the police nor the local authorities could find anything by which to identify him. Witnesses told the police that the man often walked that stretch of road, was homeless, and occasionally asked for money. The man had died alone. It was his time. They found in his pocket a set of rosary beads. The following Sunday, the local priest asked for volunteers to come to the funeral of a man with no known name, no home, and no known family. The parish church was filled with people that day. They came—busy professional types, the elderly, parents who had dropped their children at school, and many others. The church was full because there was something about him that mattered. In death as in life, dignity comes first. Pastoral ministry, indeed.

REFLECTION QUESTIONS FLOWING FROM THESE STORIES

- What touched your heart in each story?

- Who has been a pastoral minister to you? To whom have you served as a pastoral minister, either at the parish or in your life at home?

- Describe the experience of helping to heal the hearts of others, helping them to forge a connection with the Holy, or helping others as they seek holy wisdom, either at the parish or in your life at home.

- Who is being served by pastoral ministry in your parish? Who needs to be served better?

- How do you enact pastoral ministry in your everyday life?

1b. Pastoral Ministry

The Parish Meeting

1. Opening Prayer

Pray aloud together.

O God, we know that you are with us
and that you are present in all we do.
As we gather to build your Church
by the Light of the Holy Spirit,
may we be generous and kind with each other,
and open to where you will lead us.
Through Christ, our Lord. Amen.

2. Collecting Our Thoughts

1. If you haven't done so, view the video clip about pastoral ministry:

   https://pastoralplanning.com/ppmw-1
2. Invite each participant to share their definition of pastoral ministry from the preparatory section above.
3. Invite participants to share ideas from their reflection time:
   a. their experience of being ministered to or being a minister to someone else
   b. how they feel pastoral ministry is unfolding at the parish.

   Encourage people to include stories from their daily lives at home, work, or school.

3. Conversation

FAITH SHARING & DISCUSSION

1. For each of the principles of pastoral ministry listed below, discuss the reflection question or other related questions.
   a. Read each principle out loud.
   b. Hold a general discussion in the group.
   c. If your group is large, you may want to break it into smaller ones.
   d. If you have several groups, please invite each small group to share a brief report.
2. As you proceed, brainstorm specific steps you can take as a parish to deepen your impact in pastoral ministry. Write these in the space provided under "Next Steps" below.

Make notes here as you discuss

THE PRINCIPLES OF PASTORAL MINISTRY

From Promise and Hope: Pastoral Theology in the Age of Mercy, *Bill Huebsch:*

Encounter with Jesus Christ. All pastoral ministry is aimed at helping others know Christ and love the Church. It is to introduce people to the incredibly good news that we are loved and forgiven. It is to recognize the presence in our lives of the radiant and luminous Christ who—figuratively speaking—walks with us every day. That indwelling presence of the Beloved and Anointed Christ drives our prayer and lights our days and nights.

- How does your ministry as a parish lead people to know Christ and love the Church?
- How does your parish assist those who have not yet had a personal encounter with Jesus?

Sinners leading sinners. We who enact pastoral ministry are forgiven and loved unconditionally by Jesus. We are sinners leading other sinners to the Lord. We who work in this ministry must never forget our sinfulness, keeping that before us, as we learn in Psalm 51:3: "For I know my transgressions and my sin is ever before me." It is this reality that forms us as ministers of mercy. Since God has treated us with such mercy, who are we to withhold mercy from others?

- How are the people in your parish experiencing mercy from you?
- How can they be sure they will be treated mercifully and compassionately when approaching you?

A personalist theology. The encounter with Jesus is always a person-to-person experience. Each person is on a unique journey of faith. For this reason, we do not apply the law of the Church to everyone equally, for example, but we consider each case in light of the individual's conscience in a concrete situation. In pastoral ministry, the seeker doesn't encounter law or rubrics or tradition, or even theology. The seeker encounters in us a real, breathing human being, and through us, they also meet Christ. It's always personal.

- How do you treat everyone as an individual rather than merely one of a large group? For example, young parents with children preparing for the sacraments: how do you offer each parent accompaniment in their unique life situation?

Liturgy as source and summit. In the liturgy, we gather in love and solidarity. This is where Jesus stands among us as teacher, healer, and friend. It's "the source and summit of our lives" (*The Constitution on the Liturgy*, 10). As we accompany seekers on their journey, the goal is full, active participation for everyone in the liturgy. Much of our spiritual growth comes from looking over our shoulders at the repeated and ongoing experience of liturgy to see in it what gifts we have been given and to whom or what we are called. Everyone must be welcome.

- How do you help everyone return to or participate in the liturgy?

✱ Who is not welcome now, and how can you change that?

✱ How is liturgy given primary attention in the parish?

Make notes here as you discuss

The Paschal Mystery. Christ has demonstrated for us the power of self-giving, dying to self. Everyone involved in pastoral ministry—the seekers, their associates, and the companions in accompaniment—is called to die to self in this same way. And only in such self-giving do we experience the happiness and sense of well-being—even in the midst of sorrow or difficulty—that comes from knowing and walking with Christ (figuratively speaking). Entering into this dying and rising helps us know that we are children of God (Romans 8:16).

✱ How do you help everyone know and understand how to mirror and live by the paschal mystery? In particular, how do you help families embrace this way of Christian living?

God is still speaking. God is still speaking to us. It's amazing and remarkable that the Author of our very Being, yes, God, who is the Holy Mystery, with the Anointed and Beloved Christ, along with Holy Wisdom, fills us with the Spirit. God is communicating Godself to each of us in Scripture, liturgy, the depths of our conscience, our experience of love, and even the wind in the pine trees or the sound of the ocean. Through discernment, we can hear the voice of God in our lives. Every. Single. Day.

✱ How are you helping people hear the voice of God as it echoes in our world and their lives?

✱ How do you offer people the companionship of accompaniment to discern their consciences?

Grace. This self-giving of God to us, the continual way in which God authors our very Being, the gifts of Holy Wisdom poured into our hearts, the empowerment we experience when needed most, the sense of divine enlightenment—all of that is what grace is made from. It is a free and generous gift from God. It is personal to each of us while also shared among us. Grace is handed to us through our daily experience of love, the sacraments and life of the Church, and experiences of beauty, music, and shared meals.

✱ How do you clarify to everyone that grace is being offered to them, and how do you assist folks in responding to this offer?

4. Next Steps

What specific, concrete steps can your parish take to create a more open and welcoming community where pastoral ministry can occur? Consider who will do each of these, how you will fund it, and whom you hope to reach with your expanded pastoral work.

2a. Synodality

Walking Together as a Parish and Enacting Communal Discernment

If possible, please prepare for the parish meeting with the material below.

SYNODALITY

Outcome: You will understand the meaning of the term "synodality" as it's being used in the Church today. You will also understand how the enactment of "the spirit of synodality" unfolds at the parish level.

1. Prayer

Use the prayer on the "Prayer Before Each Exercise" handout or use a prayer of your own making.

2. Definition in Plain English

What is synodality? What is "acting in a synodal spirit?" How is it enacted in the Church?

1. View the video clip about synodality:

   https://pastoralplanning.com/ppmw-2

2. Learn this definition well enough to teach it to others.

Definition in plain English

Acting in a synodal spirit means that we agree to walk with each other as parishioners to lead the parish and shape how we announce the Good News. It means that we agree to both speak up and listen well as we share in decision-making through our parish and finance councils in the parish. We agree to seek more and better ways to bring the gospel to the modern world. We each agree to participate in such parish-wide communal discernment, asking what God wants for our parish. A synodal church is a church that listens… in which everyone has something to learn.

EXERCISE

Cover up the definition above and write it in your own words in the space to the right.

3. Learn about Synodality

A synod is a meeting of bishops (sometimes also including cardinals and the pope) convened to tackle issues and questions that arise among the people of God. Parishes do not have synods—they are held only among bishops—but we want parishes to learn to act with "a synodal spirit."

Pope Francis has urged that parishes go to where people live to consider how the parish can serve those who are hurting, alienated, or disconnected from parish life. Here's what he taught in *The Joy of the Gospel*, #49:

> "Let us go forth, then, let us go forth to offer everyone the life of Jesus Christ. Here I repeat for the entire church what I have often said to the priests and laity of Buenos Aires: *I prefer a church which is bruised, hurting and dirty because it has been out on the streets, rather than a church which is unhealthy from being confined and from clinging to its own security* (emphasis mine)."

The focus of our communal discernment is always outward-looking. It may also be necessary to discern internal parish matters in order to make your outward ministry effective.

This journey in a synodal spirit is one we make together. A significant part of having a synodal spirit is to listen to each other. In our age, people often come forward with strongly held opinions and rigid positions about the Church, theology, orthodoxy, and liturgy. But when we walk together, we learn to temper our own opinions to hear those of people with different experiences of the church than we have had. These others are also our companions because no one is excluded from being a companion with Jesus.

REFLECT AND SHARE

Looking back through the text above, identify two or three principles for parish synodality you could apply to your parish. For example, one might be: "To listen to each other with open hearts and minds, to learn what God is calling us to become." What are some others? Write them on the left.

LEARN FROM CHURCH TEACHING

From Pope Francis, Address to the Italian Episcopal Conference, *Synod Hall (22 May 2017), summarized*

To "walk together as a parish" is the constitutive way of the Church. It's how we interpret reality with the eyes and heart of God. This is how we best follow Jesus and become servants to one another in this wounded time. The breath and the pace of our walking together show what we are. How we learn to work together [as a synod would] shows the depth of our communion and animates our decisions.

From Cardinal Michael Czerny SJ, January 6, 2021

"One of the most innovative aspects of Vatican II's *Constitution on the Church* is the recovery of the doctrine on the 'common priesthood of the faithful' (#10), in which the laity is once again understood to be central in the life of the Church. By virtue of baptism, all her members are awarded the 'dignity of children of God,' and their active participation in the mission of the Church is proven necessary and indispensable."

From Pope Francis, Address at the Ceremony Commemorating the 50th anniversary of the Institution of the Synod of Bishops *(17 October 2015)*

"A synodal Church is a Church that listens. We realize that listening 'is more than simply hearing.' It is a mutual listening in which everyone has something to learn. The faithful people, the college of bishops, the Bishop of Rome: all listening to each other, and all listening to the Holy Spirit, the 'Spirit of truth' (Jn 14:17), in order to know what he 'says to the Churches' (Rev 2:7)."

SYNODALITY

LEARN FROM THE CATECHISM

From articles 91-92 & 783-786

All the faithful of the Church
share in the understanding
as well as the handing on of revealed truth.
Everyone who is baptized has been anointed by the Spirit
who now works within their hearts to guide them.
When all the People of God,
including the bishops and all the faithful,
understand a matter of faith or morals
with one mind and heart
they cannot be in error.
Christ was anointed.
He prayed as a priest, a person of holiness.
We're all called to that holiness.
He taught as a prophet, a wisdom figure.
We're all called to be people of Holy Wisdom.
He served as a servant ruler.
We're all called to serve each other.
Once we enter the People of God
through faith and baptism,
all Christians share in Christ's priestly vocation.
Indeed, we are consecrated in love
to be a spiritual house and a holy priesthood (of the laity).
We also share in Christ's prophetic work
especially when we echo the faith in our lives
and give witness to others.
And we share in Christ's work as servant rulers.
Christ served us in everlasting love
even though it cost him his life.
Likewise for us, we serve best when we stick to love,
and do not lord it over others,
or hoard the Church's wealth,
or choose rubrics and rules over love.

REFLECT AND SHARE

What strikes you as important in the text of the Catechism *just above? Jot down your thoughts in the space on the right.*

Add your own ideas here:

SYNODALITY

4. Enacting Synodality

Read & reflect:

The terms synod, synodal, and synodality are new to us. They're terms we don't use daily, and they might seem strange and undefined. Here are some possible ways to describe what they mean:

- We walk together as companions who form the people of God.
- We listen to one another as we choose our pathway forward as a parish.
- We share in one parish mission which requires that everyone share in shaping and stating that mission.
- It is a fundamental dimension of being church. It defines a new way of proceeding for the Church as people of God. It changes who "we" are because in a synodal church, everyone from the pope to the laity are equals in the communion of the faithful. We all have the same responsibility regarding the Church's identity, vocation, and mission.
- We open our hearts to parish members who experience church differently than we do.
- We are all responsible for parish life, but share that with others.
- We create a process in which we can all share for making decisions and completing the work. For this purpose, we use the pastoral and finance councils of the parish to convene us and process the insights of all.
- We deal with conflict with charity, honesty, and more charity.
- We can't expect that every impulse or idea from every parishioner is a good one that we must take forward.
- We learn how to discern what it is to which God is calling us as a parish. *For more on discernment, see that exercise.*
- Each of us must commit to dialogue and consensus rather than "getting our own way" or settling for "majority rule" outcomes.
- We look beyond the "regulars" we often see at the parish to set our sights on the marginalized, poor, and disenfranchised around us.

5. Synodality in Parish & Daily Life

Stories from a fellow pastoral minister:

After 24 hours of grueling travel, I landed red-eyed in New Zealand. When I arrived at the center where my conference would be held, I was greeted by the Haka. The indigenous Māori people welcomed me with a brutal dance of grotesque facial expressions. Spears in hand, their gestures were aggressive; how would I respond? A young warrior stepped forward and laid before me a small fern. The moment fell silent. What was I to do? "Pick it up," my driver whispered. Tentatively I leaned forward, picked up the fern, and the Māori people cheered. I was ushered forth into a great banquet as their guest. When I inquired about what had just happened, my wise host informed me that if you pick up the gift, you make yourself vulnerable to attack. In short, to pick up the gift is also to lay down your weapons. Likewise, in synodality. If you turn up to any meeting armed, unable to lay down your agenda, preconceptions, and prejudices, you will not achieve synodality. Lay down the weapons in your mind. This is how it begins.

Stories from a fellow pastoral minister:

If you go to Sellersburg, Indiana, you'll find the friendly parish of St Joseph's. I went there a while back to lead a retreat. During my visit, a parishioner approached me and asked, "Do you see anything unusual about our reredos?" I gazed for a while at the large wooden feature behind the altar. Three statues stood on it: Saint Joseph in the center and Saints Patrick and Boniface on either side. These latter two represented the Irish and German immigrants who had built the Church. "Look at the statue of St Boniface," I was instructed. The Germans, mainly carpenters, had built a slightly higher plinth on which their patron St Boniface could stand, making him higher than St Patrick. "They became competitive," she said, "Each wanting the higher position for their patron." Then came her wisdom: "We keep it as it is as a reminder to us how small we can become if we don't pay careful attention to each other."

REFLECTION QUESTIONS FLOWING FROM THESE STORIES

- What touched your heart in these stories? What message did the story convey to you?

- How do we need to treat each other if we are to become a truly synodal parish?

- What is your experience of being consulted and listened to in the Church—or when was that not the case and you felt overlooked or even ignored? Be as honest as possible.

- In your own words now, how would you enact "a spirit of walking together in your parish?" How do you envision holding assemblies in your parish hosted by the pastoral and finance councils, in which matters of concern to all are discussed and discerned?

- What's already happening in your parish regarding consulting everyone about priorities and other parish challenges? What would you like to see happen?

2b. Synodality

The Parish Meeting

1. Opening Prayer

Pray aloud together.

O God, we know that you are with us
and that you are present in all we do.
As we gather to build your Church by the Light of the Holy Spirit,
may we be generous and kind with each other,
and open to where you will lead us.
Through Christ, our Lord. Amen.

2. Collecting Our Thoughts

1. If you haven't done so, view the video clip about synodality:

   https://pastoralplanning.com/ppmw-2

2. Invite each participant to share their definition of synodality from the preparatory section above.
3. Invite participants to share ideas from their reflection time:
   a. their experience of being consulted, listened to, and trusted in the parish—and also those times when they were not consulted, listened to, or trusted.

   b. how your parish is now working in "a spirit of synodality" or walking together as companions, and ways in which it isn't.

   Encourage people to include stories from their daily lives at home, work, or school.

3. Conversation

FAITH SHARING & DISCUSSION

1. For each of the principles of synodality listed below, discuss the reflection question or other related questions.
   a. Read each principle out loud

   b. Hold a general discussion in the group

   c. If your group is large, consider breaking it into smaller ones

   d. If you have several groups, please invite each small group to share a brief report
2. As you proceed, brainstorm specific steps you can take as a parish to deepen your impact in synodality. Write these in the space provided under "Next Steps" below.

Make notes here as you discuss

THE PRINCIPLES OF SYNODALITY

Christ and the Eucharist. We keep Christ at the center of our entire parish project, especially as we meet him in the Eucharist and serve him "in the streets." The priests, leaders, team, and parishioners have ways to share and grow in their faith, allowing the Spirit to guide us individually and corporately.

✱ How do we live this principle as a parish? As individuals?

✱ Do we need better ways to help people grow in their relationships with Christ?

The Pastor. The pastor or parish priest (or possibly the non-ordained parish leader) embraces the spirit of synodality: walking together in the parish. He or she is the first collaborator.

✱ How do we live this principle as a parish? As individuals?

✱ Are there misgivings from your leaders that could derail us being more synodal?

The Team. The parish team, including key volunteers, works with a style of shared leadership with the pastor and parishioners. No one works in a silo of their own. Decisions are made with transparency.

✱ How do we live this principle as a parish? As individuals?

✱ Are there areas where we can improve this?

What God wants for us. Parish leaders and members frequently pause to consider to what or to whom God is calling us as a parish. This becomes our mission. This occurs within councils, committees, and working groups.

✱ How do we live this principle as a parish? As individuals?

✱ Do we need to improve how we discern together what we believe is our true mission?

Dialogue. We understand how to dialogue with each other about parish matters, including delicate ones. We honor and trust one another as dialogue partners.

✱ How do we live this principle as a parish? As individuals?

✱ Are we able to do this? Do we need help to improve our dialogue skills?

✱ Does anyone feel left out of the parish conversation?

Disagreement. We handle conflict and competing priorities with charity and honesty, both within our meetings and outside of them.

✱ How do we live this principle as a parish? As individuals?

✱ Are we good at avoiding camps? Do we honor everyone's point of view?

✱ Do our meetings dissolve into "parking lot" post-meeting discussions where people say what they failed to say within the meeting?

The Councils. We foster well-functioning parish and finance councils and hold frequent elections to name members to them.

✱ How do we live this principle as a parish?

Communication. The pastor, teams, and leaders communicate well with the wider parish.

✱ How do we live this principle as a parish? As individuals?

Those on the margins. Leaders reach out to the people on the margins of the parish whom we don't see very often at Sunday Mass or who feel otherwise alienated. We offer them mercy, understanding, compassion, and a warm welcome.

✱ How do we live this principle as a parish? As individuals?

✱ How do we communicate with those on the margins of the parish?

Feedback. We create a way to welcome feedback and input from parishioners, teaching everyone to speak with charity and to hear without becoming defensive.

✱ How do we live this principle as a parish? As individuals?

Parish-wide assemblies. Occasionally or when a major question lies before us, we assemble everyone in the parish to invite their input. Such assemblies form the annual or semi-annual method we use to hear the needs, priorities, discernment, faith experiences, and general *sensus fidei*.

✱ How do we live this principle as a parish?

Please name additional principles that guide your parish in the space on the right.

4. Next Steps

What specific, concrete steps can your parish take to create a more open and welcoming community where pastoral ministry can occur? Consider who will do each of these, how you will fund it, and whom you hope to reach with your expanded pastoral work.

Make notes here as you discuss

2c. Synodality

Resources

From the Pastoral Center:
http://pastoral.center/synodality

A one-stop location online to get needed resources from many Catholic publishers—including all those listed below—to start and sustain a synodal process in your parish.

From the Pastoral Center:
A Pastoral Toolkit for Synodality, The Pentecost Vigil Project

This free, comprehensive set of resources will help you start and sustain a synodal way of being parish. Written by the team of seasoned pastoral ministers at PentecostVigilProject.org.

From the Pastoral Center:
Christ Present in the Eucharist: A Synodal Parish Process for Eucharistic Revival, The Pentecost Vigil Project

This tool will help you host parish gatherings in a synodal style to better appreciate and reflect on Mass and the Eucharist,.

Synodality, Rafael Luciani (Paulist Press, 2022)

A first-rate readable text to explore a new way of proceeding in the Church at all levels, and as "a constitutive dimension of the Church." This path calls for a reconfiguration in the relations, communicative dynamics, and structures of the current institutional model of the Church.

Walking Together: the Way of Synodality, Pope Francis (Orbis, 2023)

In the words of Pope Francis himself: "Synodality is not a chapter in an ecclesiology textbook, much less a fad or a slogan to be bandied about in our meetings. Synodality is an expression of the Church's nature, her form, style, and mission."

Walking Together: A Primer on the New Synodality, Moira McQueen (Twenty-Third Publications, 2023)

A basic introduction to synodality and how average Catholics can take part.

A Church Renewed: 30 Days with Pope Francis on the New Synodality (Twenty-Third Publications, 2023)

A booklet with thirty reflections on synodality in the words of Pope Francis.

3a. Discernment

Learning to Hear the Voice of God Echo in our Depths

If possible, please prepare for the parish meeting with the material below.

Outcome: You will understand the meaning of discernment as it is used in a synodal process. You will also learn how enacting discernment differs from enacting a vote in a parliamentary or democratic process—and how one approaches both personal and communal discernment.

DISCERNMENT

1. Prayer

Use the prayer on the "Prayer Before Each Exercise" handout or use a prayer of your own making.

2. Definition in Plain English

What is discernment, and how do you experience it? How does a parish engage in communal discernment as it seeks to act in a synodal spirit?

1. View the video clip about discernment:
   https://pastoralplanning.com/ppmw-3

2. Learn this definition well enough to teach it to others.

Definition in plain English

Discernment is a prayerful way for us to come to relative certainty concerning what it is to which God may be calling us. In discernment, we give conscious attention to our thoughts, desires, and feelings—some lead us to love and inner peace, while others to unrest. In the discernment process, we consult "sources of wisdom," including our daily walk with Christ and the texts of Scripture, the church's teaching, our conscience, the wisdom and advice of others, and the signs of the times.

Discernment may happen about both personal and communal matters, including major life decisions, significant new directions for the parish, and other turning points. But it also happens—more often—in the daily moments of our lives as we encounter our children, neighbors, spouse, friends, and co-workers.

EXERCISE

Cover up the definition above and write it in your own words in the space to the right.

3. Learn about Discernment

As we walk through a discernment process, the Word of God is the light for our path. We must integrate it in faith and prayer and put it into practice. We take our questions into conversation with Jesus as he "walks" with us in our daily lives. We must also examine the questions in our hearts before the Lord's Cross. How are we called to die to self rather than exalt ourselves? How are we called to love our neighbors as we love ourselves? And finally, in discernment, we are aided by the gifts of the Holy Spirit, especially the gift of counsel, which helps us to judge how best to act almost by intuition. We are aided in discernment by the witness or advice of others.

From The Joy of Love, *#311-312, emphasis mine*

"Sometimes we find it hard to make room for God's unconditional love in our pastoral activity. We put so many conditions on mercy that we empty it of its concrete meaning and real significance. ...For this reason, we should always consider 'inadequate any theological conception which in the end, puts in doubt the omnipotence of God and, especially, his mercy.'

"This offers us a framework and a setting that helps us avoid a cold bureaucratic morality in dealing with more sensitive issues. Instead, it sets us in the context of a *pastoral discernment filled with merciful love, which is ever ready to understand, forgive, accompany, hope, and above all integrate...* That mindset should prevail in the Church and lead us to 'open our hearts to those living on the outermost fringes of society.'"

A HOPE AND A CAUTION

- Learning how to listen to that echo within us and trust that we can perceive to what God may be calling us in our specific circumstances allows the rich experience of our consciences to guide us.
- But a thin process of discernment can result in people following a course that merely implements their whims and selfish ambitions without regard for the deeper call of God which is always to love.

REFLECT AND SHARE

How do you hear God speaking in the church, in your life, in nature, or in other ways? How does offering people mercy and love change the tone of pastoral ministry? Who would feel more welcome and comfortable with a more welcoming, merciful tone? How does "pastoral discernment" fit into our ministry, according to Pope Francis? Write your thoughts to the left.

4. Enacting Discernment

Read & reflect on when discernment is needed, adding additional situations on the right:

Add your own ideas here:

PERSONAL SITUATIONS

* When living with and learning to love our spouse, family, and neighbors
* When changing jobs or careers
* When deciding to get married—or not
* When choosing how to handle your wealth in light of the world's poor
* When you realize the need for the care of our planet
* When you face difficulties in how to respond to a family member with whom you have a disagreement

COMMUNAL SITUATIONS

* When immigrants move into the neighborhood of your parish and you want to respond to their needs
* When you have a drop in income and need to cut the budget
* When inactive parishioners ask for the use of the building for personal use
* When setting long-range parish priorities and goals
* When deciding as a parish how to respond to discrimination and racism

5. Discernment in Parish & Daily Life

REFLECTION QUESTIONS

* What key decisions in your life or your family's life have you "discerned" through reflection, prayer, advice from others, or by speaking and listening with one another?
* Likewise, and just as importantly, what small, everyday decisions and direction do you reach as you share life with others?
* What decisions might your parish face in which communal discernment could play a role?

3b. Discernment

The Parish Meeting

1. Opening Prayer

Pray aloud together.

O God, we know that you are with us
and that you are present in all we do.
As we gather to build your Church
by the Light of the Holy Spirit,
may we be generous and kind with each other,
and open to where you will lead us.
Through Christ, our Lord. Amen.

DISCERNMENT

2. Collecting Our Thoughts

1. If you haven't done so, view the video clip about discernment:

   https://pastoralplanning.com/ppmw-3

2. Invite each participant to share their definition of discernment from the preparatory section above.
3. Invite participants to share ideas from their reflection time:
   a. their reflections about discernment: Encourage people to share stories from their personal lives "outside of the parish."
   b. discuss together how widely known and understood discernment is within the parish.

For the purposes of the conversation in this exercise, we will only discuss communal discernment within the parish. As you proceed, please remember these points:

- We seek the consensus of the faithful
- This is not the same as a democratic or parliamentary vote with winners and losers but leads to a true consensus
- The People of God are endowed with the gifts of the Spirit for these decisions, and all should be welcome to participate

Make notes here as you discuss

3. Conversation

FAITH SHARING & DISCUSSION

1. For each of the stories about discernment below, discuss the reflection question or other related questions.
   a. Read each story out loud.
   b. Hold a general discussion in the group.
   c. If your group is large, you may want to break it into smaller ones.
   d. If you have several groups, please invite each small group to share a brief report.
2. As you proceed, brainstorm specific steps you can take as a parish to deepen your impact in discernment. Write these in the space provided under "Next Steps" below.

Stories from a fellow parish minister:

St. John's has always been a parish with a balanced budget. Each year as budget time rolled around, the parish considered possible expenditures in education, liturgy, pastoral care, social concerns, and building maintenance. Once all the needs were considered, they approved an annual budget. It always kept within the range of its expected income. However, after the COVID pandemic, many parishioners have not returned to regular attendance or giving. Now the parish is facing some serious financial questions. There are insufficient funds, and the parish may have to terminate some programs and reduce overall services, but they fear that even fewer people will participate if they do. They aren't sure what to cut or how to raise more money.

✱ In the spirit of walking together in the parish, how would you create a way to discern what direction the parish should take?

Stories from a fellow parish minister:

St. Joan of Arc is a parish that has seen a huge change in its membership over the past ten years. Once a parish of mainly Irish and Polish immigrants, it is now much more diverse, including Hispanic immigrants, newcomers from various African nations, a handful of gay folks, and a sizeable group of senior citizens. The old priorities of the parish—perpetual adoration, the Polish Club, a strong focus on the parish school, and monthly bingo parties—seem out-of-date to some of the new leaders, while the long-time members have said they feel quite satisfied with the status quo. The parish priest isn't sure what to do. Up to now, he has continued supporting the old priorities, but he fears losing membership if some adjustments aren't made. He and his small team aren't sure how to proceed.

✱ In the spirit of walking together in the parish, how would you create a way to discern what direction the parish should take?

Stories from a fellow parish minister:

St. Mary Magdalene parish, known locally simply as "the Mag" is a very large, suburban parish made up mainly of people who moved out of the city center to raise their children and live in a safer neighborhood than is possible in the inner city. Many parishioners commute more than an hour each way daily. Everything seems "fine" at the parish except that the pastor and his team struggle to get people involved in any parish activities ranging from attending Mass on Sunday to social events to adult education nights to the Stations of the Cross in Lent. Many parents have told the team that parish activities conflict with hockey or dance practice and other family and school priorities. The team has detected a low level of personal faith, and no renewals of any kind have been possible for a decade. They aren't sure what to do next.

✱ In the spirit of walking together in the parish, how would you create a way to discern what direction the parish should take?

Make notes here as you discuss

DISCERNMENT

4. Next Steps

What specific, concrete steps can your parish take to create a structure and listening process in which people help discern to what God may be calling you as a parish community? Consider who will do each of these, how you will fund it, and whom you hope to reach with your expanded pastoral work.

3c. Discernment

Resources

From the Pastoral Center:
http://pastoral.center/discernment
A one-stop location online to get needed resources from many Catholic publishers on discernment—including all those listed below.

The Discernment of Spirits: An Ignatian Guide for Everyday Living, Timothy Gallagher (Crossroad: 2012)
An excellent resource for learning about discernment, with a separate reader's guide. Very well written and filled with examples.

God's Voice Within: The Ignatian Way to Discover God's Will, Mark Thibodeaux SJ and James Martin SJ (Loyola Press, 2010)
Spiritual director Mark E. Thibodeaux, SJ, shows us how to use Ignatian discernment to access our own spiritual intuition and understand that the most trustworthy wisdom of all comes not from outside sources, but from God working through us.

From the Pastoral Center:
The Catholic Way: Discernment, Ann Naffziger
This practical resource offers talking points for a group session introducing discernment along with a reproducible handout.

4a. Evangelization

Learning How to Invite and Welcome People in Christ's Name

If possible, please prepare for the parish meeting with the material below.

Outcome: You will understand the meaning of the term evangelization and how the enactment of evangelization fits into various elements of parish life. You will also examine your own life for how you have been evangelized.

1. Prayer

Use the prayer on the "Prayer Before Each Exercise" handout or use a prayer of your own making.

2. Definition in Plain English

What is evangelization? How is it enacted in the Church?

1. View the video clip about evangelization:
   https://pastoralplanning.com/ppmw-4

2. Learn this definition well enough to teach it to others.

Definition in plain English

To evangelize is to invite and welcome people into God's family at whatever level of participation is currently possible for them. It is also to guide each person to an intimate personal encounter with Christ. It is to help others understand and experience first-hand—to really *hear*—the unbelievably good news that Christ gave us> Namely that God loves us and has always loved us. That Christ walks with us (figuratively speaking) every day, forgiving us tenderly. And that the Spirit of Wisdom lives in our hearts.

EXERCISE

Cover up the definition above and write it in your own words in the space to the right.

3. Learn about Evangelization

Evangelization done well leads people to a personal encounter with Jesus Christ. This encounter is life changing. We come to realize that Christ—now a radiant, luminous presence among and within us—loves and forgives us without rejection, judgment, or punishment. This intimate encounter with the divine presence fills us with love, hope, and inner peace, no matter how dire our outward circumstances. This is the hallmark of being evangelized.

As an evangelizer, you are someone who lives your faith convincingly and speaks about it when the time is right—without annoying others. When should you speak? Only your intuition can tell you that. Others see the happiness, peace, and rightness of your life and want it for themselves. They may ask about your faith or your way of living—and such an inquiry may begin on a very small, tentative level. Over time, others will grow in love, peace, and hope, even if they haven't joined a parish. We trust that faith is dawning in their lives on a divine schedule, unfolding at whatever speed is right for them.

Following the Way of Jesus leads to having a heart for the poor, caring for those who suffer, being people of mercy, forgiving others even when they take our actions for granted, making a sacrifice that goes unnoticed, persevering in love, doing an act of kindness for someone, or dying to self as we love others.

LEARN FROM POPE FRANCIS

From The Joy of the Gospel, *#10:*

"[A]n evangelizer must never look like someone who has just come back from a funeral! Let us recover and deepen our enthusiasm, that 'delightful and comforting joy of evangelizing, even when it is in tears that we must sow… And may the world of our time, which is searching, sometimes with anguish, sometimes with hope, be enabled to receive the good news not from evangelizers who are dejected, discouraged, impatient, or anxious, but from ministers of the Gospel whose lives glow with fervor, who have first received the joy of Christ.'"

REFLECT AND SHARE

Use the space on the left to write your reflections on these questions.

- How have you encountered Christ?
- How does "walking with Christ" in your daily life affect your sense of well-being, your relationships, and the lens through which you view the world around you?
- If you don't think you have yet experienced an encounter with Christ, what attracts you to it?

LEARN FROM THE GOSPELS

- The entire mission of Jesus can be summed up in the words of Jesus from Luke's Gospel: "I must proclaim the good news of the kingdom of God... for I was sent for this purpose" (Luke 4:43).

- Jesus went from town to town to preach the message of God's saving love to the poor as well as to the religious leaders of his community.
- Jesus was the first evangelizer: he proclaimed the reign of God and the amazing Good News of God's love, mercy, and forgiveness for all.

LEARN FROM THE CATECHISM

From articles 904-906

Everyone who is baptized is called
to witness and teach about the faith
and we call this "evangelization."
And everyone is likewise called to invite others
to encounter God,
to live with Christ who reveals this love,
and to allow the Spirit of love to fill them.
Such witnessing is carried out in the ordinary circumstances
of daily life in the world.
but may often also include speaking of Christ.
Inviting others to share in this lovely church
is done by how we live, but also sometimes more explicitly.
Lay people may also be capable and trained
for specific ecclesial ministries
including catechesis
teaching theology,
and helping the Church in other ways.

LEARN FROM POPE FRANCIS

From The Joy of the Gospel, *#3*

"I invite all Christians, everywhere, at this very moment, to a renewed personal encounter with Jesus Christ, or at least an openness to letting him encounter them; I ask all of you to do this unfailingly each day. No one should think that this invitation is not meant for him or her, since 'no one is excluded from the joy brought by the Lord.' The Lord does not disappoint those who take this risk; whenever we step toward Jesus, we realize that he is already there, waiting for us with open arms.

"Now is the time to say to Jesus: 'Lord, I have let myself be deceived; in a thousand ways, I have shunned your love, yet here I am once more, to renew my covenant with you. I need you. Save me once again, Lord, take me once more into your redeeming embrace.' How good it feels to come back to him whenever we're lost! Let me say this once more: God never tires of forgiving us; we are the ones who tire of seeking his mercy."

REFLECT AND SHARE

- To what is Pope Francis calling us here?
- What parts of this text strike you as vitally important?
- Reread the second paragraph. What does this prayer say to you?

4. Evangelization in Parish & Daily Life

Stories from a fellow pastoral minister:

Tina and Charlie had quite a bit of money, several million dollars, in fact. They both had high-paying jobs and were living the high life—pretty much for themselves. John had known them for ten years or more. He began to invite Tina and Charlie to join him as occasional volunteers at a local food shelf serving the immigrant Hispanic community. John never said a single word about Jesus, his parish, his faith, or any other element of the church. But over time, both Tina and Charlie became more generous, giving gifts to the food shelf and other local charities, and understanding their wealth as a gift to be shared. Their unspoken hunger for a more spiritual life also came into focus. They never joined any church or became religious in any way, but their hearts were opened as they met the poor.

Stories from a fellow pastoral minister:

George joined the RCIA out of the blue one year. He had belonged to no church and saw himself as a secular guy who did not need faith. He had known his neighbor, Rita, for several decades, and she was his reason for joining RCIA now. Day after day, week after week, he watched Rita minister to the sick, care for her mother, and reach out to the neighbors. When a family of immigrants moved into an apartment near the local park, he noticed that she brought them clothing and donated a table and chairs from her basement. Why did she do this? he wondered. He slowly connected her loving actions toward others and her regular visits for prayer at the local church. He wanted what she had.

Stories from a fellow pastoral minister:

Martha Ann watched as her husband, Phil, lived his faith for 25 years. In all those years, Phil never asked her to become Catholic or take on any element of life in the parish. Still, out of a desire to show her love for him, Martha Ann often went with Phil to Mass on Sunday mornings. She knew that he limited his parish involvement because of her even though he would have enjoyed being part of the parish council or education committee. But mostly, she noticed that he had a great heart for the poor, a deep love for her, an ability to sacrifice himself for their shared life, always putting her first, and a remarkable willingness to forgive others and hold nothing against anyone. She knew his faith empowered him for this, and Martha Ann wondered how she could become like that.

REFLECTION QUESTIONS FLOWING FROM THESE STORIES

- What touched your heart in each story?

- What strikes you about how evangelization touches peoples' lives in each of the stories above? What is your story of evangelization?

- Who has evangelized you? Have you ever spoken about your faith to others? Has anyone ever asked you about your faith?

- How have you seen evangelization unfold in your parish?

- How have you seen it unfold in the wider culture around you? Which other religious groups are recognized for their evangelization ministries?

- Who do you know that you might like to invite and welcome into a life of faith? In your family? Among friends, neighbors, or co-workers? On the wider stage of politics, religion, and culture? Or who do you think sees your life of faith and wants to emulate it?

4b. Evangelization

The Parish Meeting

1. Opening Prayer

Pray aloud together.

O God, we know that you are with us
and that you are present in all we do.
As we gather to build your Church
by the Light of the Holy Spirit,
may we be generous and kind with each other,
and open to where you will lead us.
Through Christ, our Lord. **Amen.**

2. Collecting Our Thoughts

1. If you haven't done so, view the video clip about evangelization:

   https://pastoralplanning.com/ppmw-4

2. Invite each participant to share their definition of evangelization from the preparatory section above.
3. Invite participants to share ideas from their reflection time:
   a. their experience of being evangelized or of inviting and welcoming someone else
   b. how they feel evangelization—now a major goal of the whole church— is unfolding at the parish.
4. Discuss together how widely known and understood evangelization is within the parish. What do most people think is meant by the term?

Encourage people to include stories from their daily lives at home, work, or school.

Make notes here as you discuss

3. Conversation

FAITH SHARING & DISCUSSION

1. For each area of parish ministry listed below, discuss the reflection question offered below the list. This could become a very long discussion, but it is essential to talk through because evangelization is the church's central mission. If needed, choose several ministries for today and schedule another meeting to continue the discussion with the remaining areas.
   a. Hold a general discussion in the group, moving down the list of reflection questions for each area of ministry.
   b. If your group is large, you may want to break it into smaller ones.
   c. If you have several groups, please invite each small group to share a brief report.
2. As you proceed, brainstorm specific steps you can take as a parish to deepen your impact in evangelization. Write these in the space provided under "Next Steps" below.

AREAS OF MINISTRY

- Sunday liturgy
- Baptism preparation
- Preparation for first Reconciliation and first Eucharist
- Confirmation preparation
- Pre-school and elementary catechesis
- Junior and senior high catechesis and youth ministry
- Marriage preparation
- Adult education and lifelong learning
- Pastoral care in hospitals and care homes and all other areas of pastoral care
- Service to the poor and homeless
- Newcomers to the parish, including immigrants
- Those who seek justice in light of racism, sexism, or homophobia
- Those who work for world peace
- Those who work to draw attention to climate change
- The parish school
- Other areas of our ministry?

For each area of ministry listed above, ask yourselves these questions. As you go, please pull out specific concrete ideas and add them to the list below.

1. How well does this area of ministry in our parish "evangelize" or "invite and welcome people?"
2. How well do we introduce people to the parish as they experience our ministry in this area?
3. How do we fail to make this happen? What are our weaknesses as a parish?
4. What steps to improve might we take? List the steps in the space provided below.
5. What challenges do we face from ourselves as leaders, from the larger church, from the people of the parish, and from the culture around us?
6. What would you like to see happen here? What is your dream for this parish in this area of ministry regarding evangelization?

Also, pay special attention to those who may feel least welcome:

✱ Pay special attention in each area of ministry to those whom we see at the parish only infrequently or who have seemed to drop out.

✱ Pay special attention to Catholics living in irregular situations in terms of their primary domestic relationships, including single parents, divorced and remarried couples, ecumenical and interfaith couples, gay and lesbian couples, single adults, widows and widowers, divorced parents raising children, and others.

Make notes here as you discuss

4. Next Steps

What specific, concrete steps can your parish take to create a culture of evangelization in your parish, one through which everyone will be called beyond the liturgy and education programs to encounter Christ and walk with him in their daily lives. Consider who will do each of these, how you will fund it, and whom you hope to reach with your expanded pastoral work.

4c. Evangelization

Resources

From the Pastoral Center:
http://pastoral.center/evangelization

A one-stop location online to find outstanding resources from many Catholic publishers—including all those listed below—to learn about and enact evangelization.

http://pastoral.center/leadership-evangelization

A similar one-stop shop where you will find resources from many Catholic publishers, for leaders. Top notch collection and easy to access.

http://pastoral.center/hospitality-and-welcome-ministry

Again, an excellent location to find all the various resources from many Catholic publishers, needed to invite and welcome people to a deeper Christian life.

From the Pastoral Center:
How to Invite and Welcome in God's Name Parish Leader Kit

This free kit will help you start and sustain a culture of evangelization in your parish.

From the Pastoral Center:
Room at the Inn: Pastoral Planning Kit to Prepare for Christmas Visitors, Paul Canavese & Ann Naffziger

A practical, pastoral resource to help you especially to prepare to welcome people whom you only see in Mass at the holidays.

The Joy of the Gospel Reading Guide, Bill Huebsch (Twenty-Third Publications, 2014)

A booklet giving an overview of the apostolic exhortation Pope Francis published shortly after being elected Pope. It provides the vision that empowers us as Catholics and Christians to embrace all those who seek deeper faith.

Divine Renovation: Bringing Your Parish from Maintenance to Mission, James Mallon (Twenty-Third Publications, 2014)
Divine Renovation Group Reading Guide (Twenty-Third Publications, 2015)

These two resources provide a framework and program to implement a parish-wide renewal in which the encounter with Christ is given a prominent role.

Alpha (http://alpha.org/catholic-context/)

A parish renewal process that will help you provide the sacred moment of encounter with Christ for many people in your parish.

From the Pastoral Center:
Sanctus: Parish-based Retreat

Do you want to set your parish on fire with the love of Christ? This easy-to-use parish retreat provides everything you need to gather folks and spend a day or two on retreat together, building a core of leaders in the parish who will keep the fire burning.

From the Pastoral Center:
The Catholic Way: Evangelization, Ann Naffziger

This practical resource offers talking points for a parish session introducing evangelization along with a reproducible handout.

5a. Catechesis

Echoing the Faith with Our Lives and Our Words

If possible, please prepare for the parish meeting with the material below.

Outcome: You will understand the meaning of the term "catechesis" and how the enactment of catechesis fits into various elements of parish life. You will examine your own life for how you have experienced catechesis both in a classroom-like setting and through "formation in the world."

1. Prayer

Use the prayer on the "Prayer Before Each Exercise" handout or use a prayer of your own making.

2. Definition in Plain English

What is catechesis? How is it enacted in the Church?

1. View the video clip about catechesis.
   https://pastoralplanning.com/ppmw-5

2. Learn this definition well enough to teach it to others.

Definition in plain English

In short, catechesis is the handing on of the faith from one person to another, one generation to the next. The first message of every catechist must always be the kerygma. This handing on can be done by example, teaching, or in liturgy, but it continues throughout one's life. While once considered something only children need, today we see that all Christians need catechesis at every age and stage of life.

The *kerygma* is the core message of the Good News proclaimed by Jesus during his ministry and handed on to us. It is that God loves you and has always loved you. Jesus cares for you and knows you intimately. He demonstrated his love by his self-giving death on the cross. Now he is here among us and dwelling within us in a radiant and luminous presence. He walks with us, figuratively speaking, every day of our lives.

EXERCISE

Cover up the definition above and write it in your own words in the space to the right.

3. Learn about Catechesis

BECOMING ADULT CHRISTIANS OF MATURE FAITH

Catechists make clear the message of the kerygma. The hearer of that word may open his or her heart to faith through an encounter with Christ. Such an action is called an "initial conversion," through which we give ourselves to him. The role of lifelong catechesis is to mature that initial moment of enlightenment, deepen it, and help us speak of it to others.

- Where are you on this life-long journey?
- Share about your initial encounter with Christ and how you have kept the flame of that fire alive or how it may have gone dim.

THE LITURGY AS CATECHESIS

An essential form of catechesis is to be part of the Sunday Assembly. By taking part in the liturgy, even if one is not yet ready to take part fully, one learns the local parish's ways, spirit, and culture. The gathering, welcome, readings, homily, offering of self, Eucharistic prayer, kiss of peace, communion, community announcements, and sending forth all teach us about our faith every time we experience them.

- How does liturgy offer you continued formation in your faith, or how does it tend to disappoint and alienate you?

TEACHING AND WITNESS AS CATECHESIS

Another very common form of catechesis is to explain the faith or give instructions in it. Such teaching must be accompanied by the personal relationship of the catechist with the learner. In that companionship, the learner sees that his or her teacher lives the Way of Jesus: with forgiveness, generosity, a heart for the poor, the care of the sick, a warm welcome for immigrants, and a deep, daily devotion to Abba, the beloved Divine Presence.

- Tell the story of your religious education from childhood onward. Share about the role your family played in your formation.

ECHOING THE FAITH

Hence, we allow the teachings of Jesus to echo loudly in our lives. In this way, others can see and understand in their own lives what we profess in ours. We explain or teach only what is not made clear in that echo.

From The Joy of the Gospel, *#164, emphasis mine:*

1. "On the lips of the catechist, the first proclamation must ring out repeatedly: 'Jesus Christ loves you; he gave his life to save you; and now he is living at your side every day to enlighten, strengthen and free you.'

2. "This first proclamation is called 'first,' not because it exists at the beginning and can then be forgotten or replaced by other more important things.
3. "It is first in a qualitative sense because it is the principal proclamation, the one which **we must hear again and again in different ways**, the one which we must announce one way or another throughout the process of catechesis, at every level and moment.
4. "For this reason, too, 'the priest—like every other member of the Church—ought to grow in awareness that he himself is continually in need of being evangelized.'
5. "We must not think that the kerygma gives way to a supposedly more "solid" formation in catechesis. ***Nothing is more solid, profound, secure, meaningful, and wisdom-filled than that initial proclamation of the kerygma.***
6. "All Christian formation consists of entering more deeply into the kerygma."

The official document that directs all we do in catechesis quotes the above section of *The Joy of the Gospel* and then goes on to teach that "Kerygmatic catechesis, which goes to the very heart of the faith and grasps the essence of the Christian message, is a catechesis which manifests the action of the Holy Spirit, who communicates God's saving love in Jesus Christ and continues to give himself so that every human being may have the fullness of life" (*Directory for Catechesis, #2*).

WHAT CATECHESIS MEANS

From The Joy of the Gospel, *#166:*

"Catechesis is a proclamation of the word and is always centered on that word. Yet, it also demands a suitable environment and an attractive presentation, the use of eloquent symbols, insertion into a broader growth process, and the integration of every dimension of the person within a communal journey of hearing and response."

From The Joy of the Gospel, *#168:*

"As for the moral component of catechesis, which promotes growth in fidelity to the Gospel way of life, it is helpful to repeatedly stress the attractiveness and the ideal of a life of wisdom, self-fulfillment and enrichment. In light of that positive message, our rejection of the evils which endanger that life can be better understood. Rather than experts in dire predictions, dour judges bent on rooting out every threat and deviation, we should appear as joyful messengers of challenging proposals, guardians of the goodness and beauty which shine forth in a life of fidelity to the Gospel."

Add your own ideas here:

4. Enacting Catechesis

Read & reflect on times and places when we enact catechesis,

Possible ways to describe catechesis:

- Demonstrate what we believe by how we live
- Speak with conviction in defense of the poor and weak
- Give to others from our own money and things that they most need
- Teach systematically about what we believe using a classroom and a textbook
- Gather parents and children together and coach parents to form their own kids' faith using a resource designed for that
- Care for the sick, dying, and homebound
- Be a person of prayer but do not make a public show of that
- Speak from our hearts about compassion, mercy, and love
- Use multi-media ways of teaching, including websites, messaging, and others

5. Catechesis in Parish & Daily Life

Stories from a fellow pastoral minister:

We were caught up in "going through the motions" because we had to. It had become clear that most of them were being confirmed to please their parents. I could see that I wasn't dealing with genuine curiosity. The program we followed seemed to consist of answers to questions they weren't asking. Finally, there was a breakthrough. Seated with his legs outstretched and his hands behind his head, he said as if to challenge, "Dave, do you believe all this?" Priceless. It was what we needed. Now the catechesis could begin. A former Cardinal in England and Wales once said, "Young people don't want to know what we believe. They want to know what it means to us—only then will it begin to mean something to them." No program can substitute for the catechist because it is not until we believe in people that we can believe in what they say. Sooner or later (hopefully sooner), we will put the program down, take a deep breath, and begin the only story we can tell with authenticity: what it is that we believe and the reason for our hope!

Stories from a fellow pastoral minister:

After I left home for the first time, I began to reflect on my life with my parents. Other students gave a very different account of growing up than I did. One night, I phoned my dad to say "Thank you." I hadn't been much fun to live with in those last few years, and it was time to grow up. After fumbling my way through the call, my dad responded, "You don't need to thank us, Dave." He continued, "If you learned anything from us, the best compliment you can pay us is to give it to your children." In this gentle way, he'd given me a wise definition of catechesis. If we are careful, we can make the world a better place simply by handing on what is good and letting go of what is not. Our tradition decrees that we can learn from everything—the right and the wrong—and try to pass on the truth, goodness, and beauty that we encounter. Slowly and without seeing it, the whole world can be healed.

REFLECTION QUESTIONS FLOWING FROM THESE STORIES

* What touched your heart in these stories?

* Who has taught you about faith? Who has witnessed this faith to you by the way they live?

* How do you tell others what you believe and the reason for your hope?

* How do you pass on the truth, goodness, and beauty around you?

5b. Catechesis

The Parish Meeting

1. Opening Prayer

Pray aloud together.

O God, we know that you are with us
and that you are present in all we do.
As we gather to build your Church
by the Light of the Holy Spirit,
may we be generous and kind with each other,
and open to where you will lead us.
Through Christ, our Lord. Amen.

2. Collecting Our Thoughts

1. If you haven't done so, view the video clip about catechesis:

   https://pastoralplanning.com/ppmw-5

2. Invite each participant to share their definition of catechesis from the preparatory section above.
3. Invite participants to share ideas from their reflection time:
   a. their experience of being catechized or being someone who offered catechesis to others, and
   b. how they feel catechesis is unfolding at the parish.

   Encourage people to include stories from their daily lives at home, work, or school.

3. Conversation

FAITH SHARING & DISCUSSION

1. Discuss the reflection questions for each of the three "challenges" listed below.
   a. Read the challenge out loud.
   b. Hold a general discussion in the group.
   c. If your group is large, you may want to break it into smaller ones.
   d. If you have several groups, please invite each small group to share a brief report.
2. As you proceed, brainstorm specific steps you can take as a parish to deepen your impact in catechesis. Write these in the space provided under "Next Steps" below.

Make notes here as you discuss

THE CHALLENGES IN CATECHESIS TODAY

The Encounter with Christ Precedes Catechesis. And yet, we often leap into "education" or "teaching" both adults and children without regard to their level of conversion to Christ.

Discussion:

- What do we mean when we speak of "an encounter with Christ?"
- Why do we often start with teaching?
- How can we offer people such an encounter with Christ as the "first step?"

Notes for your discussion:

- While such an encounter cannot be forced upon anyone, we can provide the context in which we know such an encounter often occurs.
- Such a context can be created by:
  a. always beginning with faith sharing
  b. offering parish-based retreats (see the resource list)
  c. providing at-home resources for prayer
  d. making available the witness of people who've already had an encounter
  e. what other ways?
- What is your parish plan to provide these moments of encounter?

Parents Have the Primary Voice in the Formation of Their Children. And yet, parents are often encouraged or required to "drop off" their children at the parish. They go shopping or wait in the parking lot while a volunteer catechist—often a stranger to them and their children—catechizes the child. We know this doesn't work but continue to enact it yearly.

Discussion:

- Why doesn't substituting parish volunteers for parents work?
- How do children learn and grow in faith?
- How can we coach parents to be the teachers of their own children?

Notes for your discussion:

- There are enjoyable and effective ways to coach parents as they become the primary ones forming their children's faith. The parish can plan to provide these opportunities to parents. Such opportunities are life-changing for the children, the parents, and the parish.
- See the resource list for examples called "Growing Up Catholic."

- What specific steps will we take in this parish to coach and support parents as the primary voice passing the faith to their children?

Make notes here as you discuss

Catechesis is not Meant Mainly for Children but is a Life-Long Process. And yet, most parish plans and budgets—indeed, most parish personnel—are aimed only at children. For children's formation to really take hold and be effective and long-lasting, we know that the whole parish must be a community of learners. There are powerful and effective ways for us to establish inter-generational and life-long learning in the parish.

We also know that, when the whole parish participates in learning, everything in the parish grows: participation, donations, prayer, new members seeking a lively parish, and service to the poor.

Discussion:

- What forms of lifelong or adult learning could we adopt as a parish?
- As we said above, how can conversion or an encounter with Christ be the first step?
- How can faith formation for life become a primary objective of our parish?

Notes for your discussion:

- There are excellent, easy-to-use, parish-based retreats available to implement that provide opportunities to encounter Christ. See the resource list for examples.
- A principal way people encounter Christ is by faith sharing. How can you build such faith-sharing into every gathering at the parish?
- How will we take specific steps to offer lifelong and inter-generational learning in this parish? When will we start this? Who will lead it?

4. Next Steps

What specific, concrete steps can your parish take to offer catechesis at every age and stage of life, particularly for young parents? Consider who will do each of these, how you will fund it, and whom you hope to reach with your expanded pastoral work.

5c. Catechesis

Resources

From the Pastoral Center:
http://pastoral.center/adult-faith-formation

A large collection of outstanding resources from all the Catholic publishers to help you organize and enact a strong lifelong faith formation process in your parish.

http://GrowingUpCatholic.com

A home base for Growing Up Catholic resources designed to accompany and coach parents to form their own children in faith.

From the Pastoral Center:
Fashioning Faith

An extensive online subscription service packed with creative resources for intergenerational faith formation.

Growing Faith, Bill Huebsch (Twenty-Third Publications: 2023)

A set of twelve booklets presenting the core teachings of the *Catechism of the Catholic Church* in plain English. The resource is pastoral, easy to use, and especially easy to facilitate.

From the Pastoral Center:
Why Coach Parents? Leader Resource Kit

This free, versatile kit is the ideal resource for use within your parish or school to begin the process of shifting from "doing it for parents" to "coaching them to do it themselves." The "it" here is forming their own kids with the faith of the church: passing that faith on to the next generation.

From the Pastoral Center:
Growing Up Catholic Sacramental Preparation

There is no other sacrament preparation program like this one. It accompanies parents to form their own children and prepare them. In the process, the parents have their faith renewed and their connection to the parish strengthened.

From the Pastoral Center:
How to Lead Faith Sharing

This free guide explains how to use a Question of the Week and Breaking Open the Word process to integrate faith sharing into any parish gathering.

6a. Accompaniment

Understanding the Companionship of Accompaniment as a Key Element of All Pastoral Ministry

If possible, please prepare for the parish meeting with the material below.

Outcome: You will understand the meaning of the term "accompaniment" as it's being used in the Church today and how the enactment of accompaniment might unfold at the parish.

1. Prayer

Use the prayer on the "Prayer Before Each Exercise" handout or use a prayer of your own making.

2. Definition in Plain English

What is accompaniment? How is it enacted in the Church?

1. View the video clip about accompaniment:
   https://pastoralplanning.com/ppmw-6

2. Learn this definition well enough to teach it to others.

Definition in plain English

Accompaniment occurs when one Christian becomes a companion to another to help that seeker pay attention to what God might be asking of him or her in a specific situation in life. In "the companionship of accompaniment," we walk with each other, listening without judgment or rejection. We help each other form, listen to, and follow our conscience. By this method, we help each other find a home in the family of God.

EXERCISE

Cover up the definition above and write it in your own words in the space to the right.

3. Learn about Accompaniment

In spiritual accompaniment, we guide each other along God's pathway. We extend to one another the unbelievable and life-changing truth that God forgives us completely. Accompaniment also leads us to become God-like. We call each other to be more forgiving, more generous, less judgmental, less greedy, more loving, more enthused, less harsh, less full of lust, and closer to the heart of Jesus.

THE MYSTERY OF GOD

No one can plumb the mystery of God's presence in another person's life. Therefore, we must listen carefully to how God calls each person to himself (*The Joy of the Gospel*, #171). It goes without saying that we who accompany others must learn the art of listening, which is more than simply hearing. To listen is to have an open heart; this leads to genuine encounter and intimacy in Christ.

HOW GOD CALLS US

A good companion in accompaniment can also find the right gesture and word at just the right moment when it is time to speak, offering the one being accompanied a gentle nudge toward God's heart. One who accompanies others must realize that each person's relationship with God is a mystery. God calls us in ways that often surprise us and may not be fully understood. A companion in accompaniment, therefore, is not an intrusive judge who scolds and condemns but a true companion who has reverence for the mysterious ways in which God may be working in the life of the other (*The Joy of the Gospel*, #172).

A well-trained companion "invites others to let themselves be healed, to take up their mat, embrace the cross, leave all behind, and go forth ever anew" (*The Joy of the Gospel*, #172). We learn as accompanists to be patient and compassionate with others, as we hope they will be with us.

REFLECT AND SHARE

In your own words, summarize what you hear Pope Francis teaching us about pastoral ministry. Use the space on the left.

THE ART OF ACCOMPANIMENT

From The Joy of the Gospel, *#169:*

"In our world, ordained ministers and other pastoral workers can make present the fragrance of Christ's closeness and his personal gaze. The Church will have to initiate everyone—priests, religious and laity—into this 'art of accompaniment' which teaches us to remove our sandals before the sacred ground of the other."

"No one can be condemned forever," Pope Francis reminds us, "because that is not the logic of the Gospel!" (*The Joy of Love*, #297).

CONSCIENCE

In an accompanying parish, the team understands that "conscience can do more than recognize that a given situation does not correspond objectively to the overall demands of the Gospel. It can also recognize with sincerity and honesty what for now, is the most generous response which can be given to God and *come to see with a certain moral security that it is what God himself is asking amid the concrete complexity of one's limits*, while yet not fully the objective ideal" (*The Joy of Love*, #303, emphasis mine).

REFLECT AND SHARE

Write your response to the following reflections in the space to the right.

* Looking back over the text you just read, identify two or three principles about accompaniment that could guide your parish as it undertakes this form of pastoral work. For example, one might be: "To be God-like means to forgive people their offenses as God would: completely, immediately, and lovingly."
* What other principles can you draw from this material?

4. Enacting Accompaniment

WHO IS WAITING FOR THE COMPANIONSHIP OF ACCOMPANIMENT?

All sorts of folks populate our parishes. Many live in the mainstream of parish life. Still, others dwell on the margins of the parish because of their marital or household situation, doubts about their faith, a long absence from Sunday Mass, unresolved hard feelings with a pastor or fellow parishioner, or other reasons. Who are these people?

Add your own ideas here:

Read & reflect on when accompaniment is needed:

* Couples who aren't active but who ask for baptism, first communion, or confirmation for their child
* Newcomers who haven't been made to feel welcome yet
* Divorced and remarried couples and their extended families
* Cohabitating couples and their friends and families
* Gay or lesbian couples and their associates
* Those who are in a crisis of faith
* Women who feel that the Church does not respect or trust them and their vocations
* People who have a theological difference with the Church
* Immigrants who don't speak the principal language of the parish
* The poor who feel they don't have the right clothes or are otherwise embarrassed to be present

- People who feel that the changes in the Church after Vatican II ignored their desire for traditional devotions.
- Ecumenical couples who don't feel the parish welcomes or respects the faith of the non-Catholic.

5. Accompaniment in Parish & Daily Life

Stories from a fellow pastoral minister:

It was a six-hour drive to our home on the south coast of England. After three hours, it was time for a comfort break. We were tired. For the most part, our journey had been quiet. We spent the time listening to music. The two of us are not normally short of things to say, but we sat comfortably in our silence, tired, thinking about the week ahead. As we pulled up, I turned the engine off, and as I reached for the car door, he said to me, "Dad, I think I'm in love." Then, as though pondering his own statement, he added, "What do you think love is?" When I look back now and think about that moment, it's how we sat in the car that strikes me. This is not the sort of question you ask when you are looking at someone. It's a question you ask when you're side-by-side, shoulder-to-shoulder. Geography is important. The honest, deep questions we ask in search of meaning and truth are rarely asked in a classroom, seminar, or parish hall. They're usually asked in a parking lot or out on a long walk, in a conversation of equals.

REFLECTION QUESTIONS FLOWING FROM THIS STORY

- Think about who are your life's companions and note those you accompany or whom you accompany. Write their names or initials in the space below.
- Who in the Church has offered you companionship and accompaniment over the years?
- Who do you know who feels judged or rejected by the parish or church leaders?
- To whom are you a companion in accompaniment?

6b. Accompaniment

The Parish Meeting

1. Opening Prayer

Pray aloud together.

O God, we know that you are with us
and that you are present in all we do.
As we gather to build your Church
by the Light of the Holy Spirit,
may we be generous and kind with each other,
and open to where you will lead us.
Through Christ, our Lord. Amen.

2. Collecting Our Thoughts

1. If you haven't done so, view the video clip about accompaniment:

   https://pastoralplanning.com/ppmw-6

2. Invite each participant to share their definition of accompaniment from the preparatory section above.
3. Invite participants to share ideas from their reflection time:
   a. Who has offered you accompaniment?
   b. How was Jesus a primary model of accompaniment? Think of the stories of him as a companion to others on the road to Emmaus, with Zacchaeus, with the woman caught in adultery, or calling Matthew the tax collector, among others.
   c. How widely known and understood is accompaniment within the parish?

   Encourage people to include stories from their daily lives at home, work, or school.

Make notes here as you discuss

3. Conversation

FAITH SHARING & DISCUSSION

1. Discuss each step in the unfolding of accompaniment as it is presented below.
    a. Read each accompaniment step and its description out loud
    b. Hold a general discussion in the group
    c. If your group is large, you may want to break it into smaller ones
    d. If you have several groups, please invite each small group to share a brief report
2. As you proceed, brainstorm specific steps you can take as a parish to deepen your impact in accompaniment. Write these in the space provided under "Next Steps" below.

HOW DOES ACCOMPANIMENT UNFOLD?

We begin by announcing that all are welcome in the parish. We invite people to come and join us regardless of their situation in life. Then we offer them the companionship of accompaniment to help them sort out how they can become committed, fully incorporated parish members.

In our parish, how would this first step unfold?

✱ What is needed? What obstacles do we face? What first step can we take?

Decision. First, we agree together as a parish that we want to offer everyone such companionship. This decision includes the pastor, team, and in the spirit of synodality, the whole parish.

✱ Have we reached this decision as a parish?

✱ What else must we do to ensure this decision is final and well understood by the whole parish?

Planning. Once we have decided to move forward as an accompanying parish, we must examine each area of parish ministry and write up some notes for a pastoral plan.

✱ Who might benefit from such companionship?

✱ How can each area of ministry offer accompaniment?

✱ What role should generally be played by the parish priest, especially where the sacrament of reconciliation is needed?

✱ What steps could we take immediately to open wide our doors and welcome all the People of God into our family?

Skills. At the same time, we must learn the method and art of accompaniment. Many people already have these skills and are standing by, ready to use them for the parish's mission.

Make notes here as you discuss

- How will we create a training process to help everyone learn this art?
- In time, this should include families, youth, school teachers, catechists, pastoral care workers, and others—but to get started, who is ready to undertake this ministry and with whom?
- How can we help people develop these needed skills?
  a. Attentive, non-judgmental listening
  b. Theological reflection with the seeker
  c. A good knowledge of church teaching
  d. An understanding of the role of conscience
  e. The skills for discernment for the seeker

Get Started. Becoming a parish where the companionship of accompaniment is practiced begins with each pastoral moment, each homily, and each occasion of reaching out to seekers in need. It begins slowly and builds with the pastor and team's constant support, training, and encouragement.

- What are our first steps? (Please clarify them once again here to make sure everyone understands them. List them below.)

A COUPLE OF CAUTIONS

- When we accompany others, our role is not to get someone into reaching some forgone conclusion. We are always helping them to make their own discernment. As Pope Francis says, "We have been called to form consciences, not replace them."
- Entering into companionship with each other can be very helpful, but sometimes we need more than a companion—we need a counsellor, mentor, spiritual director, or confessor to help us enter deeply into the discernment needed to follow the way of Jesus.

4. Next Steps

What specific, concrete steps can your parish take to create a community where those seeking to return or take their place among us are accompanied with pastoral sensitivity and mercy? Consider who will do each of these, how you will fund it, and whom you hope to reach with your expanded pastoral work.

6c. Accompaniment

Resources

From the Pastoral Center:
http://ArtOfAccompaniment.com
This website is a one-stop shop for resources from many Catholic publishers, all aimed at helping you understand and enact accompaniment in your parish.

The Art of Accompaniment: Four Essential Conversations on Becoming the Kind of Parish the Church Needs Today, Bill Huebsch (Twenty-Third Publications: 2017)
How to Become an Accompanying Parish Powerpoint Planning Process, Bill Huebsch (The Pastoral Center: 2017)
These tools are the perfect way to get started with accompaniment in your parish. The *Art of Accompaniment* booklet can be used in small groups or alone and is structured with study and reflection questions to help you start and sustain the ministry of accompaniment in your parish. The associated planning process adds a visual presentation and leader notes.

The Joy of the Gospel Reading Guide, Bill Huebsch (Twenty-Third Publications, 2014)
Chapter eight, in particular, focuses on accompaniment.

From the Pastoral Center:
Walking with Jesus: A Bible Study for Learning the Art of Accompaniment, Art Zannoni, Ann Naffziger, and Paul Canavese
Through this four-session faith-sharing process for any parishioner, let Jesus teach you how to accompany others through his example.

7a. Theological Reflection

Prayerful Reflection Helps Us Hear What God May Be Asking of Us

If possible, please prepare for the parish meeting with the material below.

Outcome: You will understand the meaning and practice of theological reflection as it is used in pastoral ministry. You will understand how the enactment of such theological reflection enriches and grounds the work of accompaniment, among other tasks of pastoral ministry.

1. Prayer

Use the prayer on the "Prayer Before Each Exercise" handout or use a prayer of your own making.

2. Definition in Plain English

What is theological reflection? How is it used in the ministry of accompaniment?

1. View the video clip about theological reflection.
   https://pastoralplanning.com/ppmw-7

2. Learn this definition well enough to teach it to others.

Definition in plain English

Theological reflection is a form of prayer through which we pause to carefully consider our personal experience in light of our faith. During this reflection, we discern what God asks of us in a given situation. As such, theological reflection is a principal means of connecting faith with daily life. Reflecting on our situations in life is as natural as breathing, but to do so "theologically"—with an ear to the teaching of the Church, the voice of our conscience, and the inner light of the Holy Spirit—requires intentionality and prayerfulness.

EXERCISE

Cover up the definition above and write it in your own words in the space to the right.

3. Learn about Theological Reflection

HOW DO WE ENACT THEOLOGICAL REFLECTION?

The principal activity of pastoral theology is a form of prayerful theological reflection drawing on the sources that include

(1) Scripture and friendship with Jesus,

(2) the teaching of the Church,

(3) the conscience and life experience of the seeker, and

(4) the signs of the times.

The context for the reflection is accompaniment. A person seeking help brings a concrete situation or experience, a question, decision, or concern to the pastoral accompanist and asks for help.

The companion in accompaniment—with ears open to the seeker and heart open to Jesus—invites the seeker to tell his or her story and listens with an active, non-judgmental heart. For the companion, this is the first stage of the prayerful theological reflection.

The art of sacred inquiry. Slowly the companion in accompaniment asks about the matter at hand, following a somewhat formal-yet-informal inquiry of accompaniment, bringing to bear all four sources. See the notes about this below.

Discernment for the seeker. Using however much time is needed or available—it could be a few hours, several months, or many years—the companion slowly helps the seeker discern what God may be asking of him or her in their current situation in life. This discernment shows signs along the way of either consolation or desolation on the seeker's part. The companion in accompaniment is attuned to this holy activity. The work of discernment belongs to the seeker, not the companion. *For more on discernment, see the third exercise of this process above.*

Discernment for the accompanist. However, the companion is also in the process of sacred discernment, listening to his or her own heart about what is happening and trusting the nudges and intuitions that may assist the process.

Decision. At some reasonable point, the companion in accompaniment assists the seeker in reaching a point of decision and action, which may lead to integration in the parish. This may conclude the accompaniment relationship for them.

Evaluation. Afterward, the companion and his or her colleagues evaluate and appraise the experience and process. Accompanists do not act alone but in league with others.

MORE ABOUT THE ART OF SACRED INQUIRY IN ACCOMPANIMENT

In formal theological reflection, we use a method or specific way of moving from one point to another as we pray and reflect. We refer to this method as "the art of sacred inquiry" because we are inquiring about what God may ask of the seeker. The role of the companion is to help the seeker discern this. Theological reflection may confirm, challenge, clarify, and expand how we understand our own experience and how we understand our religious tradition.

In brief, the method for sacred inquiry follows these steps:

1. The seeker tells his or her story, describing their experience to identify "the heart of the matter."
2. The companion in accompaniment listens attentively and prayerfully.
3. Together they inquire into the sources of wisdom using sacred inquiry.
   a. Those sources include Scripture, church teaching, the life experience and conscience of the seeker, the wisdom of others, and the signs of the times.
   b. Many people have not learned to hear the voice of their conscience as it echoes in their depths, but it's essential to this process.
4. This leads to insight and reflection on both their parts.
5. The seeker begins to discern what God may be asking.
6. Both are aware of their prejudices, including attitudes, beliefs, and personal history that can prevent either the seeker or the companion from hearing without being judgmental.
7. And both strive to be aware of the power of darkness that can cloud their reflection.
8. Eventually, in due time, the seeker reaches a decision.
   a. If the seeker experiences a sense of consolation in this decision, they may move forward.
   b. If the seeker's experience is one of desolation, they pause and continue reflecting together.

WHO CAN DO THEOLOGICAL REFLECTION?

You can. We all can. One doesn't need a university degree in theology to be capable of theological reflection. We can all accompany each other, offering insights and encouragement to one another. Here are the needed qualifications:

1. A close connection to the Holy One

We don't need a degree, but what we do need is a close, prayerful relationship with God as the Author of our very Being, as the source of love, and as the origin of all life. We need awareness of Christ's radiant and luminous presence within and among us, the Beloved One. We need an openness to Holy Wisdom to have our hearts filled with the Spirit. Having a degree doesn't guarantee such a prayerful posture for anyone. When we are conscious of the divine presence, we naturally become prayerful and daily prayer is essential if we are to accompany one another.

2. A close connection to the People of God

We also need a full awareness of the teaching of the Church, the People of God. This teaching is our collected wisdom, gathered through the ages, and it becomes our guide and norm as we journey through life. Knowing church teaching does not imply that we should impose it on anyone because—as valuable as it is to us—it remains only a guide. Deep within each of us is our conscience where we detect the voice of God echoing within us, and it is this voice that accompaniment helps ring clear in the lives of others (see the *Catechism*, article 1776 and following).

3. A close connection to the Living Liturgy

As companions in accompaniment, we must also be people of the liturgy. Our call is not merely to "attend" Sunday Mass but to live the liturgy in our daily lives. And this "living liturgy" is also a call to engage with the culture around us, to scrutinize the "signs of the times" because those we accompany—the seekers—are people of these times. Following the pastoral style of Jesus, in accompaniment, we withhold judgment of others to allow them to discern to what or whom God is calling them.

4. A little bit of coaching

Finally, when a prayerful member of the People of God who lives the liturgy in daily life, steps forth as a companion, a small amount of training is needed to understand the methods, limits, possibilities, and accompaniment opportunities. Again, theological reflection aims to help us learn how to respond to those who come forth as seekers, asking questions about their faith, the Church, and themselves. We want to respond to them with mercy and compassion, modeled on "the way of Jesus."

REFLECT AND SHARE

Please pause here for a brief reflection. Write your responses in the space to the left.

- Looking back over these qualifications for being a companion in accompaniment, how do you measure up?
- In your words below, list these qualifications as you understand them and note your readiness.
- Think back over your experience and tell a story or two of a time when you either accompanied someone else or were a seeker being accompanied yourself.

4. Enacting Theological Reflection

WHO MIGHT BENEFIT FROM THEOLOGICAL REFLECTION IN ACCOMPANIMENT?

Discernment and accompaniment aim to understand to what God is calling us and apply the teaching of the Church to our life situations. The situations about which we reflect might include any of the happy, sad, or confusing moments in life. For example,

1. When a divorced person (without an annulment from the first marriage) falls in love again with someone they could marry—or is already remarried—what is the way they should follow?

    ✱ A companion in accompaniment who is knowledgeable about church teaching and the life situation of this couple can help them enter into prayerful theological reflection in order to discern how to proceed.

2. When a parishioner comes forth asking for guidance in a faith crisis,

    ✱ A companion in accompaniment can help him or her walk through this moment in their lives with grace.

3. When a woman in the parish comes forth to question why the Church doesn't recognize her as a candidate for ordination or other leadership roles on a par with men,

    ✱ A companion in accompaniment can help her discern the direction she should take, or at least to understand how to respond to the vocation she is experiencing.

4. When a group of parishioners asks for more traditional devotions or styles of public prayer in the life of the parish, saying they feel left behind as parish life has become more contemporary,

    ✱ A companion in accompaniment can help them understand and appreciate how to respond to the deep calling they may be experiencing to worship and pray.

5. When there are new parishioners of any kind, including immigrants who don't speak the primary language of the parish,

    ✱ A companion in accompaniment can help them find their way into parish life, understand the culture of the parish, and feel at home there.

6. When a young couple wants their child to prepare for receiving first Reconciliation or Eucharist,

    ✱ A companion in accompaniment, using a resource designed for this, can coach this young couple to become the primary voice in the formation of their child.

In each of these examples, the companion helps the seeker bring their life situation into dialogue with church teaching, the voice of their conscience, and each person's prayerful relationship with God. Again, this is called theological reflection, and it is essential to pastoral ministry well-done. **What other situations may arise that call for the use of theological reflection to help a seeker come to know what God may be asking of him or her in a given situation?**

Add your own ideas here:

5. Theological Reflection in Parish & Daily Life

Stories from a fellow pastoral minister:

My mum had a great line for me when I was naughty as a child. It would go something like this: "Go to your bedroom and give yourself a good talking to." Even as a child, it was as if she was inviting me into an internal dialogue or "theological reflection." If I sat there for a while, my conscience would rise above my ego, and the word "Sorry" would follow shortly afterward. This is what the Church calls "an examination of conscience." Indeed, if you sit with something and ponder it, as did Mary, the mother of Jesus, you come to realize a great truth and the true reality of the situation. My mum wouldn't have called this theological reflection, but that's exactly what it was. Talking to yourself is not a sign of madness but quite the opposite. Reflection is not something we do enough of, and theological reflection is something we're just learning about now. If you don't know what to do, find a favored space and start by giving yourself a good talking to.

REFLECTION QUESTIONS FLOWING FROM THIS STORY

- What touched your heart in this story? What did it teach you about theological reflection?

- When have you paused in your life's journey to apply theological reflection to a situation? Describe how you did it. Please recall such moments of reflection and prepare to share them with the rest of your group when we meet.

7b. Theological Reflection

The Parish Meeting

1. Opening Prayer

Pray aloud together.

O God, we know that you are with us
and that you are present in all we do.
As we gather to build your Church
by the Light of the Holy Spirit,
may we be generous and kind with each other,
and open to where you will lead us.
Through Christ, our Lord. Amen.

2. Collecting Our Thoughts

1. If you haven't done so, view the video clip about theological reflection:

   https://pastoralplanning.com/ppmw-7

2. Invite each participant to share their definition of theological reflection from the preparatory section above.
3. Invite participants to share ideas from their reflection time:
   a. their experience of using theological reflection to come to terms with a life situation
   b. how they feel theological reflection could improve and enhance various parish ministries, including the sacrament of Reconciliation, confirmation preparation, home life, and the ministry of accompaniment.

Encourage people to include stories from their daily lives at home, work, or school.

3. Conversation

FAITH SHARING & DISCUSSION

1. Discuss the reflection questions for each of the five categories listed below where theological reflection might serve the church's mission.
   a. Read each description out loud.
   b. Hold a general discussion in the group. Your question for discussion is this: **How does theological reflection as Catholics affect how we might accompany people in each category?**

Make notes here as you discuss

c. If your group is large, you may want to break it into smaller ones.

d. If you have several groups, please invite each small group to share a brief report.

2. As you proceed, brainstorm specific steps you can take as a parish to deepen your impact in theological reflection. Write these in the space provided under "Next Steps" below.

THE PLACES AND PEOPLE OF THEOLOGICAL REFLECTION AS USED IN ACCOMPANIMENT

1. **Helping family members serve as companions in accompaniment for each other.** How can you use theological reflection to help families reach decisions together as a couple or the whole family, including children? They might be asking how to proceed in their lives with

   a. How to regulate the number of children and what role birth control might play.

   b. How to respond to members of their extended family (or even those who live within the same home) who are divorced, remarried, gay and perhaps married, not actively in a parish, estranged from one another, divided over politics, or other like situations.

   c. How to shift from being on the margins of the parish to a more active place in parish life, especially as the children enter religious education.

   d. How to share the family money with the poor, homeless, and hungry.

   e. What other key family questions might arise in which family members could accompany each other?

2. **Accompanying active parishioners.** How can you use theological reflection to help regular, active members of the parish sort out the questions that arise, such as

   a. How to decide what course of treatment, if any, one should follow with a diagnosis of terminal illness.

   b. How to welcome and connect with others in the parish who have different political views in a highly polarized culture such as the one we now have.

   c. How to invite and welcome friends and family who have left behind an active connection with parish life and liturgy.

   d. What other key questions might arise for regular, active parishioners?

3. **Accompaniment for people in special situations:**

   a. How can parents accompany their children?

   b. How can we in the parish accompany one another?

c. "The Irregulars." How to accompany people we know who are in "irregular" situations relative to the Church, especially those considered "most sinful," such as the remarried, gay couples, or others.

Make notes here as you discuss

4. **Accompanying inactive parishioners.** How can you use theological reflection to help inactive parishioners in moments such as

   a. When they come to request a funeral for a deceased family member, baptism or first Communion for a child, the use of the church for a wedding, and other like situations.

   b. When you learn that an inactive parishioner is sick or dying, including when you learn this accidentally in the hospital.

   c. When you see them at Christmas, Easter, weddings, or funerals.

   d. What other situations might arise in this group?

5. **Accompany people in the wider community outside the parish as such.** How can you offer the companionship of accompaniment when

   a. When there is discrimination against neighbors based on

      * racism
      * homophobia
      * being poor or unemployed
      * sexism
      * their political party
      * *what other forms of discrimination?*

   b. When you are confronted by people living in poverty (either near you or distant from you).

   c. You realize that people are fleeing from war and violence.

   d. You realize that the immigrants on your nation's border are seeking asylum, freedom from poverty, or other inhumane situations.

   e. What other like situations might arise?

4. Next Steps

What specific, concrete steps can your parish take to utilize theological reflection to help people sort out and live with the thorny life questions demanding attention and discernment? Consider who will do each of these steps, how you will fund it, and whom you hope to reach with your expanded pastoral work.

7c. Theologial Reflection

Resources

Promise and Hope: Pastoral Theology in the Age of Mercy, Bill Huebsch (Twenty-Third Publications: 2020)

In parts four and five of this groundbreaking resource, author Bill Huebsch introduces readers to theological reflection and describes how it is used in accompaniment. The same method for theological reflection is used for communal discernment in synodal decision making.

Method in Ministry: Theological Reflection and Christian Ministry, James D. and Evelyn Eaton Whitehead (Sheed & Ward, 1995)

An excellent primary source on using theological reflection.

The Art of Theological Reflection, Patricia O'Connell Killen and John deBeer. (Crossroad, 1995)

A practical guide to learning the methods of theological reflection.

8a. Missionary Discipleship

and Pastoral Planning

If possible, please prepare for the parish meeting with the material below.

Missionary discipleship is the fire burning within us that propels us into our community as heralds of the Good News.

Outcome: You will understand the meaning of the term "missionary discipleship" and how the enactment of it becomes the mission of the Church itself. You will learn about the strong connection between missionary discipleship and evangelization, ways by which we announce the kerygma.

1. Prayer

Use the prayer on the "Prayer Before Each Exercise" handout or use a prayer of your own making.

2. Definition in Plain English

What is missionary discipleship? How is it enacted in the Church? What is pastoral planning?

1. View the video clip about missionary discipleship and pastoral planning:

   https://pastoralplanning.com/ppmw-8

2. Learn this definition well enough to teach it to others.

Definition in plain English

We become missionary disciples when we have an encounter with Jesus—and his great love for us—that transforms us and sets our hearts on fire! We immerse ourselves in the Good News of the kerygma. We turn our hearts to Christ and follow him. We feel bound to share the fire of his love with others, inviting and welcoming them—when they are ready—to walk with us in the family of God.

EXERCISE

Cover up the definition above and write it in your own words in the space to the right.

Definition of pastoral planning in light of our call to discipleship in plain English:

A pastoral plan spells out how we will "go forth to love and serve Christ and one another." It is a plan for parish activity but also a plan for the personal activity of each member of the parish. Its focus is outward, not inward. We are sent out to heal the wounds of people all around us.

EXERCISE

Cover up the definition above and write it in your own words in the space to the left.

3. Learn about Missionary Discipleship

From The Joy of the Gospel, *#120, emphasis mine:*

"In virtue of their baptism, ***all the members of the People of God have become missionary disciples***. All the baptized, whatever their position in the Church or their level of instruction in the faith, are agents of evangelization, and it would be insufficient to envisage a plan of evangelization to be carried out by "professionals" while the rest of the faithful would simply be passive recipients.

"The new evangelization calls for ***personal involvement on the part of each of the baptized.*** Every Christian is challenged, here and now, to be actively engaged in evangelization; indeed, anyone who has truly experienced God's saving love does not need much time or lengthy training to go out and proclaim that love."

THE VISION FOR YOUR PARISH'S PASTORAL PLAN

How would you like to be part of a parish in which nearly everyone is on fire with the Holy Spirit and understands and embraces their call to be missionary disciples? This would be a parish where people want to share Jesus' love with others, liturgy is filled with enthusiasm, and people give from their hearts in money and ministry. This is a parish where people step forth—not to "help Father" with ministry—but as ministers in their own right because of God's remarkable presence in their lives.

Does this all sound impossible? Are you able to dream this dream? Can you envision this in your parish? What is needed for this to happen in your community?

How would it unfold? Please be specific. Who would do the work, and how would you fund it?

ENCOUNTERS WITH CHRIST THAT LEAD TO ADULT CONVERSION

The foundation of missionary discipleship is people having a way to encounter the powerful presence of Christ—now in radiant and luminous form—in their daily lives. How do we encounter Jesus in this way? Such an encounter is a powerful and life-changing moment in one's life. From that moment onward—even if we step away from conscious awareness of it—we experience the presence of the Holy within and among us. We become people of mercy, forgiveness, generosity, kindness, and self-giving love.

Read from The Joy of the Gospel, *#1 & 3:*

"The joy of the gospel fills the hearts and lives of all who encounter Jesus. Those who accept his offer of salvation are set free from sin, sorrow, inner emptiness and loneliness. With Christ, joy is constantly born anew."

"I invite all Christians, everywhere, at this very moment, to a renewed personal encounter with Jesus Christ, or at least an openness to letting him encounter them; I ask all of you to do this unfailingly each day. No one should think that this invitation is not meant for him or her, since 'no one is excluded from the joy brought by the Lord.' The Lord does not disappoint those who take this risk; whenever we take a step towards Jesus, we come to realize that he is already there, waiting for us with open arms."

In a 2015 address to the Italian Church, Pope Francis said, "We are not living an era of change but a change of era." The future of the Church is in our hands. "I desire a happy Church with [the] face of a mother, who understands, accompanies, caresses," he said. "Dream of this Church, believe in it, innovate it with freedom."

4. Enacting Missionary Discipleship with a Pastoral Plan to Drive It

Add your own ideas here:

How do we encounter Jesus and set our hearts on fire?

- We pause and turn our heart to Christ. Simply open yourself to his presence within you. Speak to him as to a friend, sharing your desires, secrets, and needs.
- We allow ourselves to spend time in quiet and silence, contemplating all the gifts we have been offered in our lives, especially those we love, the Eucharist, the beauty of nature, God's generous forgiveness, and the life, message, and continued presence of Christ in our midst.
- We make a retreat aimed at this goal.
- We follow a pattern of daily prayer in which we learn to hear the echo of God's voice within us, figuratively speaking.
- We become mindful of the indwelling divine presence.

How do we proclaim Christ's love?

- We live our lives convincingly following the Way of Jesus. When others see us, the Good News we want to announce is already obvious because of our own peace, happiness, and love.
- We speak up for the poor and weak whom Jesus loved.
- We welcome visitors, immigrants, those fleeing from war, and newcomers.
- We join and are active in a parish.
- We are people of mercy, forgiving those who offend us, offering food to those who have none, and making personal sacrifices on behalf of others.
- When someone asks about our lives and values, we share our faith.

5. Missionary Discipleship in Parish & Daily Life

Stories from a fellow pastoral minister:

After a long flight, I found myself in front of a stern-faced security officer. I had ticked the box which says I am visiting to work. Looking over his half-rimmed glasses, he says to me, "What is the nature of your visit here?" "I'm speaking at a conference," I replied. "What is the conference about?" he asked. "Oh," I stumbled, "I'm here to talk to teachers and volunteers about the importance of education." Without a change to his demeanor, he enquired about how long I'd be in the country and what I would be paid, and then, he finally stamped my passport. What I'd said to him was true, but there was more to it than that. I was there to help people encounter the love of God and, hopefully, through that, their own dignity. I'm conscious of how easy it is to disguise what I do for fear of judgment. Because I'm not an extremist, not sectarian, not homophobic, not prone to neurosis, and not carrying unscientific views about creation, I don't want to be put into those categories. It is hard to use the language of faith outside our meetings because of the prejudice we may meet. Missionary discipleship takes courage and discernment.

Stories from a fellow pastoral minister:

As so often happens during a conference, people use the break times to say something to the speaker. As someone who often finds himself in this situation, I'm never quite sure what to expect. On this occasion, a young man approached me, stared intently for a moment, and began as if he was angry. "I've been listening to you," he said. "Thank you," I replied cautiously. This could go many ways. Quite unexpectedly, his eyes welled up, and his intention turned to resignation. As though I had punched him in the stomach, his posture crumpled. "You see," he said, "I'm what you describe in your talk." He continued, "Even when I'm playing with my kids in the evening, I want them to go to bed so that I can get on with my work. I want to change that." My talk had somehow held up a mirror to this man's life, and he'd seen something he didn't like. You never know when you will be a missionary disciple for someone in need. It's not always in the parish plan.

REFLECTION QUESTIONS FLOWING FROM THESE STORIES

* What touched your heart in these stories?

* Do you consider yourself a missionary disciple? What are the signs in your life that lead to this? What challenges do you face with it?

* Who has served as a missionary disciple in your life? Who has helped you encounter Christ, helped you grow in faith, or helped you connect all of this with your regular, daily life?

* How do you imagine it would be possible for your parish to help others encounter Christ more deeply and, subsequently, to grow in faith and announce God's forgiving and loving good news to others in your neighborhood, city, or even beyond?

8b. Missionary Discipleship

The Parish Meeting & Writing the Pastoral Plan

1. Opening Prayer

Pray aloud together.

O God, we know that you are with us
and that you are present in all we do.
As we gather to build your Church
by the Light of the Holy Spirit,
may we be generous and kind with each other,
and open to where you will lead us.
Through Christ, our Lord. Amen.

2. Collecting Our Thoughts

1. If you haven't done so, view the video clip about missionary discipleship:

   https://pastoralplanning.com/ppmw-8

2. Invite each participant to share their definition of missionary discipleship and pastoral planning from the preparatory section above.
3. Invite participants to share ideas from their reflection time:
   a. their experience of being a missionary disciple or of knowing others who were
   b. how they imagine the parish could become a place of personal encounter with Christ—and a busy center of missionary discipleship as a result.

Encourage people to include stories from their daily lives at home, work, or school.

Make notes here as you discuss

3. Conversation

AS WE EMBRACE OUR CALL TO BE MISSIONARY DISCIPLES

1. Follow these steps to finish your work with a sound pastoral plan:
   a. Read the summary below out loud, with each person reading one bullet point.
   b. Next, discuss the three reflection questions leading to your pastoral plan.
   c. Finally, using the **Planning Process** outline, discuss each of the five potential new initiatives that might help you advance your pastoral ministry. You may need more than one session to complete this work. Please plan to hold follow-up meetings to conclude the work.
   d. If your group is large, you may want to break into smaller ones.
   e. If you have several groups, please invite each small group to share a brief report.
2. As you proceed, brainstorm specific steps you can take as a parish to deepen your impact in missionary discipleship and pastoral planning. Write these in the space provided under "Next Steps" below.

SUMMARY OF OUR WORK IN THESE EXERCISES

Read the summary below out loud, with each person reading one bullet point.

- The call to be missionary disciples summarizes and draws together all our work in these exercises.
- Echoing our comments in the introduction, we would say that we are a church steeped in **solid pastoral theology** and ministry.
- Our way of being together, of walking together in the parish, is **synodal**—listening and responding to the real, concrete situations in which we all live.
- We use **discernment** to understand what God asks of us as a community or as individuals.
- We know that the principle activity of the church is **evangelization**—inviting and welcoming people in Christ's name to enter the People of God at whatever level is comfortable for them at this time.
- This is what Jesus sent us to do: "Go therefore and make disciples of all nations..." (Matthew 28:19a).
- Once people are evangelized and have experienced conversion, **catechesis** can become effective at every age and stage of life.
- And for many people seeking to follow the Way of Christ but working through various life situations, we offer **companionship**

and accompaniment, employing **theological reflection** to help them sort out their questions and follow a path of holiness.

- All this work occurs, of course, within the parish context. In **liturgy, education, and pastoral care.**
- We can summarize all of this pastoral activity by that clear, loud summons to be **missionary disciples** of Jesus.
- As missionary disciples, we walk with each other in synodal ways, discerning the pathway forward, evangelizing and catechizing each other, and offering one another the companionship of accompaniment when needed.
- It's the sum of all we do as church—but we do have to plan for it, fund it, and schedule it in the parish calendar—or it will never happen.

Make notes here as you discuss

REFLECTION QUESTIONS LEADING TO YOUR PASTORAL PLAN

Discuss these three reflection questions leading to your pastoral plan.

Reflection 1: Throughout this process, you have identified various specific, concrete steps you can take as a parish to enhance and expand each area of ministry.

- Pastoral theology
- Synodality
- Discernment
- Evangelization
- Catechesis
- Accompaniment
- Theological reflection

For each of these areas of pastoral ministry, what ideas did you name as you went through the exercises? Return to them and share them with each other, writing them on a white or blackboard for all to see.

Reflection 2: Many parishes have developed a parish plan based on the ministries of

- **Liturgy** and the sacraments, including RCIA
- **Education**, including the school if any
- **Pastoral care**, including outreach
- (Sometimes, work for justice and peace)
- (Sometimes, community building)
- Plus, finances and building maintenance

For each of these existing areas of ministry in your parish, summarize your current pastoral plans. This can be a brief review. If you have this in print, please share it with all.

Make notes here as you discuss

Planning Process

Church leaders are challenging us to expand on this plan by adding ministries such as the ones below, fitting these into our existing plan. **For each of the new items below, talk together about the following practical matters:**

1. Who would lead this effort?
2. How would we tie this into our existing pastoral ministry plans?
3. How will we do this? What steps will we take?
   a. What challenges or pitfalls should we prepare for?
   b. Who will be upset or pleased by this? Who will oppose or support it?
4. How will we communicate this to the wider parish?
   a. How can we consult everyone in a synodal style about our plan?
5. How much will this cost and how will we fund it?
6. Who will do this work?
7. How will we evaluate what we're doing?
8. How will we keep the fire of this initiative burning in the parish?

Five Areas of Ministry to Expand

1. ENCOUNTER CHRIST AND OPEN WIDE YOUR DOORS.

Create a context within the parish through which people can encounter Christ and turn their hearts toward him. The needed context might be parish-based retreats of various kinds, faith-sharing, shared prayer times, or other initiatives. These encounters are what light the fire in your parish and drive **evangelization and missionary discipleship**.

✱ Pastoral theology holds such conversion as its first principle.

✱ It's essential in order for discernment to be authentic.

✱ It's the core of evangelization.

✱ Conversion precedes catechesis.

✱ It's the basis of all theological reflection.

2. LOOK OUTWARD TO INVITE AND WELCOME FOLKS TO PARISH LIFE.

Can this include full and active participation in liturgy and reform of the liturgy that welcomes, nourishes, and satisfies the spiritual hunger of participants? This might require a broader invitation to the liturgy.

* Synodality is an expression of our Eucharistic bond.
* In evangelization, many people have left because they aren't welcome.
* We really cannot catechize people who aren't at the liturgy.
* Accompaniment has restoration or welcome to full communion as its major goal.

Make notes here as you discuss

3. SYNODAL ASSEMBLIES

Parish assemblies to discuss, discern, and decide major parish questions. We will learn to listen, respond, and be flexible as we learn how God is leading people.

* Discernment plays the key role in reaching parish decisions.
* This greatly expands the role of parish councils as they host synodal assemblies.

4. LIFE-LONG FAITH FORMATION

Catechesis beyond children of elementary school age.

* Without life-long learning, synodality cannot work since it's based on knowing and understanding life in the church.
* The accompaniment of parents—the bedrock of our future—requires that we coach them to be the primary voice forming their own children.
* All theological reflection depends on people knowing their faith and being able to speak about it.

5. ACCOMPANIMENT

A plan for accompaniment of all who seek life in the church. This requires reaching out to those who are sitting at the edge of parish life—and there are more people there than in our center.

* Rather than keeping our focus on who is present, we shift our focus and reach out to those who are absent or tentative.
* This requires that we open our hearts and our doors, acting in the pastoral style of Jesus who invited people first, shared a meal with them, and called them to holiness through his friendship with them.

Your Conclusion

Write up your plan, share it widely, and then move forward.

8c. Missionary Discipleship

Resources

Forming Intentional Disciples: The Path to Knowing and Following Jesus, Revised and Expanded, Sherry A. Weddell (Our Sunday Visitor, 2022)
Becoming a Parish of Intentional Disciples, Sherry A. Weddell (Our Sunday Visitor, 2015)
These influential and insightful books highlight the gap between how many Catholics live out their faith and our call to intentional, missionary discipleship—and what ministry leaders can do about it.

Divine Renovation: Bringing Your Parish from Maintenance to Mission, James Mallon (Twenty-Third Publications, 2014)
Divine Renovation Group Reading Guide (Twenty-Third Publications, 2015)
These resources provide a framework and program to implement a parish-wide renewal that send its members out as missionary disciples.

Threshold Bible Study: Missionary Discipleship, Stephen Binz (Twenty-Third Publications, 2017)
Build a strong foundation for your parishioners by helping them understand the Scriptural roots of missionary discipleship. Discipleship is a call to go inward, to experience an ever-deepening encounter with Jesus Christ, and a call to go outward, to witness the good news to others.

The Reluctant Disciple: Daring to Believe, David Wells (Twenty-Third Publications, 2015)
The Grateful Disciple: Daring to Be Loved, David Wells (Twenty-Third Publications, 2016)
Humorous and enlightening stories of living discipleship, with commentary and questions for reflection.

The Joy of the Gospel Reading Guide, Bill Huebsch (Twenty-Third Publications, 2014)
Pope Francis calls all Christians to undertake the work of going out to the margins of society and the church to welcome and invite everyone in Jesus' name.

ALSO FROM BILL HUEBSCH & THE PASTORAL CENTER

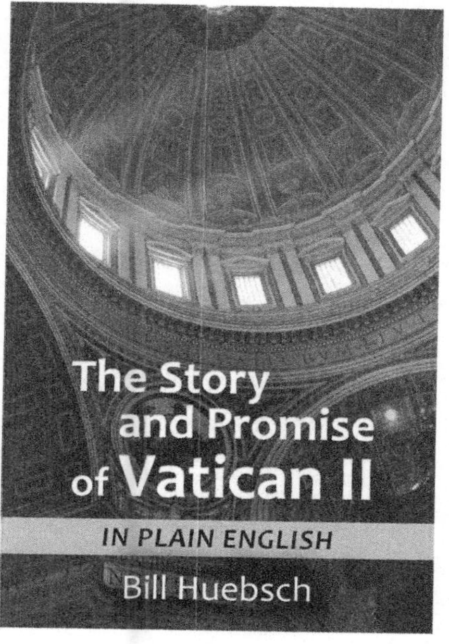

The Story and Promise of Vatican II
in Plain English

It isn't possible to prepare for or enact pastoral ministry today without being a student of Vatican II. From participatory liturgy to whole-family faith formation, from the RCIA to the diaconate, and from the renewed call to holiness to the renewed age of mercy, the springboard of the modern church is Vatican II. Because of this, knowing about the story of Vatican II is essential to understanding its promise.

This volume tells that wonderful story of the council—and it does so in plain English. It follows an exciting chronological pathway from the beginning of the council to its final bell. But the deep promise of the council is found in the documents themselves. Church documents don't always make for compelling reading but the plain English presentations which author Bill Huebsch provides here make this book a page-turner! Huebsch captures the excitement and rapidly unfolding drama—all set in the theater of St. Peter's Basilica during those four years in the early 1960s. He treats each character with dignity and respect, moving beyond the judgments of "too liberal" or "too conservative" that have dogged the Church and created division rather than unity. This book fills its readers with hope and equips them to unfold the promise of the Second Vatican Council in today's world.

Paperback book • 6" x 9" • 250 pages • WH102

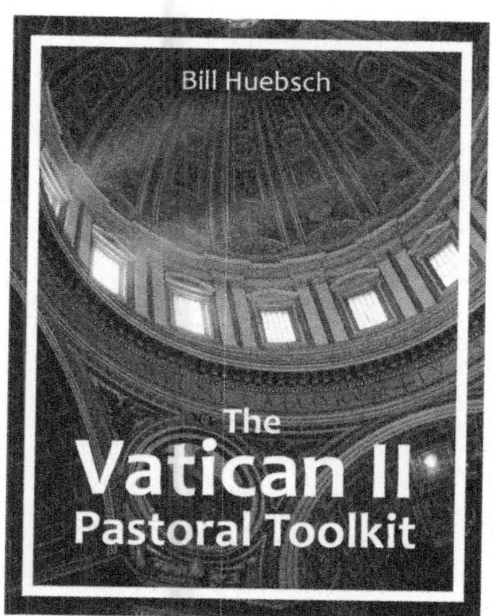

Vatican II Pastoral Toolkit
Study Guides, Videos, Prayers, Articles, Catechesis

This valuable toolkit provides a wealth of resources to help you share the message of the Second Vatican Council with your community, especially for use with his book *The Story and Promise of Vatican II in Plain English*. Pope John Paul II called Vatican II "the Advent Liturgy of the new millennium." It is vital that all parish leaders be familiar with what this council did and how the Holy Spirit moved the Church to reform itself in the work of the world's bishops and Popes.

Downloadable eResource • 8½" x 11" • 479 pages • WH103

$28/parish (free with purchase of five or more copies of *The Story and Promise of Vatican II in Plain English*)

Learn more at http://vatican2.center

Printed in Great Britain
by Amazon